Social Media for Your Student and Graduate Job Search

D0367291

Social Media for Your Student and Graduate Job Search

Marielle Kelly

 palgrave

First published 2016 by PALGRAVE

Palgrave in the UK is an imprint of Macmillan Publishers Limited, registered in England, company number 785998, of 4 Crinan Street, London, N1 9XW.

Palgrave Macmillan in the US is a division of St Martin's Press LLC, 175 Fifth Avenue, New York, NY 10010.

Palgrave is a global imprint of the above companies and is represented throughout the world.

Palgrave® and Macmillan® are registered trademarks in the United States, the United Kingdom, Europe and other countries.

ISBN 978–1–137–47237–3 paperback

This book is printed on paper suitable for recycling and made from fully managed and sustained forest sources. Logging, pulping and manufacturing processes are expected to conform to the environmental regulations of the country of origin.

A catalogue record for this book is available from the British Library.

A catalog record for this book is available from the Library of Congress.

Printed in China

Contents

CHAPTER 9
Make the most of Facebook, Pinterest, Instagram and Video CVs

Acknowledgements

I would like to thank every job seeker and student I have worked with over the years. They have all taught me so much and given me the motivation to write this book. I'm grateful to each person who has played a part in getting this book from a germ of an idea to a finished product. I particularly want to thank Úna Burns, without whose support this book would never have been written. Thank you to my family and friends who let me disappear for a while and are still talking to me, and to my colleagues for all their encouragement. Thank you also to Johnny Campbell, who first got me hooked on the incredible potential of social media to help people get to where they want to be in their careers.

Introduction: Becoming social media savvy

Contents

Social media has changed the face of recruitment. With over half of employers using social media to screen candidates when they apply, and 94 per cent using it to locate new hires, it pays to make good use of LinkedIn®, Twitter® and other social media platforms in your job search.[1] Millions of jobseekers are already leveraging social media to help them in their job search, and 73% of 18- to 34-year-olds found their last job through a social network.[2]

Why you need to be socially savvy

There's a big difference between having a social media account and being socially savvy. A basic, public Facebook® profile in which you share the gory details of what you got up to on Saturday night is not going to make employers view you as a great potential employee. Neither is a half-hearted LinkedIn page. Social media for your job search is all about connecting with people and communicating who you are and what interests you. You can do this by creating content such as updates and images, and interacting with status updates and posts created by others. You'll learn how to do all those things as you go through this book.

Managing one or more social media profile will have an impact on what employers see if they put your name into a search engine, which they are increasingly doing. Give yourself a helping hand by making sure that what they find says "Hire me" and not "Run a mile from me". Don't expect social media to be a magic wand that will single-handedly lead to jobs falling at your feet. Used correctly, however, it can be a great ally in your job search. It can help you to uncover job opportunities, meet people who can give you career advice and research information to stand out from other applicants in a crowded graduate marketplace.

The first half of this guide will take you through everything you need to know about why you should be using social media in your job search. You might be tempted to skip ahead to the second half, which details how to use key social media platforms, but it's important to get a good overall understanding of how they can help you and how to make the most of them. Chapter 1 gives you an overview of each of the main sites covered in this book and talks you through the pros and cons of each. In Chapters 2 and 3, you'll work on defining your brand and then explore how to communicate that through your social media accounts.

In Chapter 4, you'll learn how you can use social media to enhance your job search in many different ways. This chapter includes an outline of how businesses use social media in the recruitment process, which is key information if you're looking for a job. You'll also find out how to uncover more vacancies and find out more about careers through different platforms. Chapter 5 covers the importance of making connections to help you choose a career, as well as how to prepare better applications. It will guide you through finding people with whom to connect and how to do that in a way that works.

The second half of the book, Chapters 6, 7, 8 and 9, gives you a deeper understanding of major social media platforms, starting with LinkedIn and moving on to Twitter, blogging, Facebook, Pinterest® and Instagram®. You'll find out about key features of each of these sites and learn how to make the most of each platform to help you to get ahead as you set out on your search for an internship or graduate role. Whether you are a current student or a graduate, looking for a part-time job, summer internship or graduate job, the advice in these pages is for you.

Social media anxiety

Setting up your online profiles and promoting yourself so blatantly may seem daunting at first. Don't panic. You don't need to do everything at once. It's a good idea to gradually and systematically build up your online presence. Read through the chapters carefully to build your understanding of what makes a great social media profile and to build your confidence before taking the plunge.

If the thought of having too much information available about you online is holding you back, rest assured that it's completely within your control to choose how much or how little to share. Every platform allows you to set restrictive privacy settings, so you can keep things away from public view until you're happy with the profiles you have developed.

Take time to go through the exercises in this guide. They have been designed to help you get to grips with the key aspects of using social media for job searching. Have a tablet or laptop to hand as you go through this book; you'll need to go online to complete many of the exercises. All the social media platforms in this guide have mobile apps, but they tend to have less functionality than the desktop versions, so you will get a better sense of each of them on a tablet or laptop. You'll also want to check out the different websites that you will be guided through as you go along.

Companion website

For everyone

The companion website for this book includes a range of features that will support you as you go through the different elements covered here. You will find printable worksheets associated with some of the exercises. Social media is ever evolving, and the workings of each of the platforms discussed in this book have a tendency to change often. Keep an eye on the website, where you'll find up-to-the-minute explanations and details about any major changes that might occur across the platforms. You can access the companion site here: www.palgrave.com/companion/palgrave-career-skills

For educators

In addition to the worksheets available on the website, you will also find a series of free, customisable PowerPoint® presentations that you can use as a basis for class sessions with your students.

Social media for your job search

Contents

You probably use social media every day, several times a day, to connect with friends, see what people you know are up to and share your own updates and photographs with others. This is the purely social side of social media, and it might seem like this is all it can do. Look a bit deeper. There are so many ways you can use it to make your job search more effective.

If you have any social media profiles, such as a Facebook or Twitter account, you already have an online presence. That presence can work in your favour as you embark upon your search. It can also work against you. In a new hiring landscape where employers are looking up candidates online, it's in your best interest to take control of what they find. Hiring decisions can come down to a very small number of deciding factors, and social media provides a space where you can actively manage the impression you make on employers.

The end of the CV?

Social media is becoming so widely used as part of the recruitment process that the days of the CV can seem numbered. This may eventually be the case, but for now, there is a place for both. You can use your social media profiles to boost your job search in so many ways: you can apply for some jobs directly on LinkedIn through your profile, or you might send a speculative email to a prospective employer, including a link to your blog or LinkedIn page to help showcase what you have to offer. This, in turn, could lead to an interview. You could network your way into a job using your social media profiles as your calling card. Your online activity can complement traditional application documents by providing additional ways of showcasing your skills, interests and experience.

Don't be tempted to throw away your CV just yet, or to hand in a sloppy application because you feel your LinkedIn profile is impressive and should do the job. A poor CV will get thrown into the "reject" pile or screened out by an applicant tracking system, so a prospective employer may never have the chance to wonder what's available about you online. Social media is playing an ever greater role in recruitment, but companies are still using the traditional approach of assessing CVs, cover letters and application forms.

Social media platforms

There are a lot of social media platforms out there, with new ones emerging all the time. Before getting into all the ways you can make social media work for you, you need to know what the main platforms are and what each one does well. The following pages take you through the main reasons you should consider different social media sites to help you to secure an internship or graduate job.

LinkedIn

In a nutshell LinkedIn is probably the first online network that springs to mind when you think of social media and finding work. It was launched in 2003 and now hosts hundreds of millions of profiles. Individuals set up profiles outlining their professional and educational experience, and use the site to connect with other professionals and to keep track of their network. University students are one of the fastest growing demographics on the platform, so don't feel like you can't join until you're in a "proper job".

What you can post You can create a LinkedIn profile, which is like an online CV with a lot more features. It's where people can learn about your background and the work that you do or would like to do. You can also add rich media, such as photographs or PDFs of your work, to make your profile more interesting. You can post updates related to your sector on your timeline, although most public interaction on LinkedIn happens in LinkedIn groups with specific subject focuses. There are groups for all kinds of professional interests, where you can ask questions, share articles and discuss news items.

How it can help you get a job As the most prominent social network with a professional focus, LinkedIn should play a central role in your job search. The fact that you can use it to create a professional online presence is just the start. It allows you to read other people's career paths on their profiles, which is incredibly useful when you are making decisions about your next steps. You can also use the Alumni tool to find out where graduates from your course and your university have gone over the years. And it's a useful way to keep track of your network as you go through your career. There is a whole section of the site dedicated to advertising jobs, and a growing number of companies are making it possible for you to apply for roles directly through LinkedIn by submitting your profile through the site, making applications a little bit easier.

The downside The biggest stumbling block that students face with LinkedIn is that it can be very hard to know what to say about yourself so early in your career. The majority of students will have some casual work experience, perhaps an internship or two and maybe some voluntary work, in addition to their studies. This might seem like information that's not worth sharing when you compare it to the extensive profiles of other people on LinkedIn with established careers. Firstly, you're at the very start of your working life, so you're not expected to have the same breadth of experience as others on the platform. Secondly, and more importantly, there are so many ways that you can draw on your time in university and your extracurricular activities to show that you are a great candidate. It's just a matter of knowing what employers want and how to show them what you've got.

There can also be a perception that people are likely to lie on LinkedIn, to inflate their experience. However, research by Cornell University found that people were less likely to lie about their work history on LinkedIn than on their CV.[3] This makes sense, as it's riskier to lie on an online profile that is there for all to see.

Chapter 1

Employer's view: Paul Vance,
Head of Resourcing, KPMG Ireland

So many students use social media tools to their advantage nowadays by spotting internships and graduate opportunities. It can be seen as an effortless way to research a company and their activity.

KPMG places a big emphasis on use of social media during the annual graduate recruitment campaigns. We ran a recruitment campaign called Think KPMG, which was linked to our official graduate careers Facebook page. All pictures taken throughout this campaign were uploaded onto Facebook for students to like and share. We relied heavily on social media to promote this campaign. Social Media is also how we inform the students on each of our on-campus events.

Make sure you are "connected". All students should be following/friends with/ connected with all the relevant companies they could potentially secure a job with – not only on Facebook, but on Twitter, LinkedIn and, most recently, Instagram.

Twitter

In a nutshell Twitter is called a micro-blogging site, which essentially means you can use it to post short updates. You can follow accounts belonging to your friends and to people you have never met who are posting interesting tweets. In turn, anyone on Twitter can follow you to keep up to date with what you're posting, unless you set your account to private.

What you can post The site limits you to writing posts, called tweets, which are a maximum of 140 characters long. You can also tweet photographs or videos, repost tweets from other accounts and share links to articles on other websites. Twitter also allows you to interact with other users by replying to tweets or indicating that you like them through the "favourite" function.

How it can help you get a job Twitter has a mix of company accounts and individual accounts. Following companies you want to work for, and people who do the kind of work you might like to do, is a quick way of finding out what people in the sector are talking about. It's also a good way to see what companies are saying about themselves online, so you'll understand what matters to them, meaning you can position yourself as a candidate who fits with their vision. Lots of jobs are advertised on Twitter which might not be advertised elsewhere. More and more graduate recruiters are using Twitter to engage students, and some of them run Twitter campaigns, which are a great way for you to get involved with the company and get on their radar. It's also a useful networking tool where you can get to know other people working in companies and sectors you would like to target.

The downside There is so much information available at your fingertips through Twitter that you can feel bombarded. There are ways to manage this and refine the information you see, which will be covered later. It can also be a challenge to fit a clear point into 140 characters, but this doesn't take too long to master. The fact that anyone can retweet anything you post means that you can very quickly lose control over how far your tweets travel, which means you need to be particularly mindful about not sharing anything that might hurt your online brand. You can delete your own tweets, but they can still be there for all eternity in the public accounts of anybody who has shared what you have written.

Blogging

In a nutshell A blog is a website which you manage and where you can write about anything you want. You can post as little or as often as you want, be that daily or once a month. What matters is sharing interesting content and being consistent. Blogs are generally open to anyone to read, and you can enable a function which lets other readers comment on what you have written. Your blog posts can be as long or as short as you want, although shorter posts tend to be more effective.

What you can post Blogs are usually text-based, so you can write about your chosen subject, whether that's your thoughts on events on the international political stage, your interpretation of interesting historical primary sources you've come across in class, or a blog about your travels. You can also post photographs or graphics to illustrate your written work. Some bloggers choose to share only photographs with brief commentary, to highlight visual work they have created or the work of others that they admire.

How it can help you get a job Blogging might not lead directly to a job, but it can definitely be an asset in your job search. A regularly updated blog shows commitment and confidence in your opinions. If you're writing about the sector you want to go into, that can be a great way of providing evidence of your career motivation. However, a blog on a subject that is completely unrelated to the jobs you are considering can also be an asset. It shows that you have the determination to work on a project you have set yourself, and it can also be a place where you showcase your strong writing ability. Many employers specify that they require someone with strong written communication skills, and a well-written blog provides great evidence of these skills, which you can highlight in job applications.

The downside Blogging takes commitment. A blog with three posts in a week and then nothing for months does not create a particularly positive impression. In the same way that an updated blog can display commitment, an untended blog gives out the impression that you are someone who doesn't stick with what you've started. Writing a good blog post takes a lot longer than drafting a tweet or a Facebook update or pinning an image on Pinterest. So if you're going to blog, you need to set aside the time to do it right.

Facebook

In a nutshell Facebook is one of the longest-running social media platforms, launched in 2004. It's one of the most "social" of social media platforms, as it's most commonly used for staying connected with friends and family.

What you can post You can write status updates, upload photographs and videos and share links. You can also comment on the items posted by your friends and share their posts to your timeline.

How it can help you get a job Many companies, including a large number of the major graduate recruiters, have Facebook pages where they share updates about their company and news about vacancies. Some run Facebook games or competitions to get prospective employees to engage with them online. Your own Facebook profile can have an impact on your chances of finding a job, particularly if your status updates, comments and photographs are publicly available. That impact can be positive or negative depending on how well you manage what you post, and your privacy settings. It also has a little-known feature that helps you to find people you might know who are working in different companies who could be able to share insights and advice.

The downside Facebook has traditionally been used more for social purposes than for anything to do with finding work, so it's something of a shift to start thinking of it as a platform that could play a part in your job search. If you use Facebook already, there could be lots of publicly accessible photographs and comments with your name tagged on them, so Facebook could be your biggest liability in your job search if you don't review what's already out there and put it under lock and key.

My social media story: Zara McGrath, Social Media Journalist, Storyful

As soon as I finished my undergrad, I had a week's break and then immediately began a traineeship with my current employer. However, before I had received this placement, I had interviewed for another internship, and I used social media platforms to obtain the interview.

I discovered the job via Twitter. I sent a PDF of my CV that contained a hyperlink to each of my social media platforms, which I had cultivated into résumés. These included LinkedIn, Twitter, Google+®, and About.me®. During the interview the interviewer asked me questions based on information he could only have garnered from my social media profiles. I also used Twitter to search for possible jobs during that time, following accounts such as JobFairy and Journalism.co.uk.

My advice for people searching for jobs is this: don't rely solely on social media to act as your CV. Yes, LinkedIn is instrumental in making connections with people in your field but having an actual CV to hand is not something to be underrated.

Be wary of your privacy settings on Facebook. You do not want a potential employer viewing pictures of your wild Saturday night out. Your social media profiles are your public persona, so ensure that everything that can be found about you online consists of things that you want to be found. This includes every account, especially Twitter.

Pinterest

In a nutshell Pinterest is an image-sharing platform where you can create virtual pinboards and save images, or pins, according to your interests.

What you can post Posts on Pinterest are called "pins". They are images pinned from websites, so you can pin a combination of things you find on other sites and pins that Pinterest users have shared on the platform. Pinterest describes pins as virtual bookmarks, and it provides an easy and visually appealing way to keep track of interesting articles in one place. For example, if you were doing a lot of research to help you prepare for an interview, you could create a pinboard called "Interview preparation", and if you read an interesting article with interview tips, you could pin it to your boards and refer back to it at any stage.

How it can help you get a job Pinterest won't play a central role in your job search unless you are targeting a career in a creative sector like interior design, photography or fashion-related roles, but it can play a strong supporting role regardless of your career aspirations. You could create pinboards linked to your career interests, where you pin articles and infographics that you find helpful. This is another way of positioning yourself online and confirming that you are genuinely interested in a particular sector. It also means you can use it as a repository for all the useful information you come across to do with a particular job or sector, making it easy for you to keep all your research in one place and review it before an interview.

The downside Pinterest can be highly addictive. It's very easy to use, and every time you log on you are presented with images linked to things you've pinned before, so there is a constantly updated stream of interesting images to explore. As Pinterest alone will not get you a job, the fact that it can very quickly take up a lot of your time means it's dangerously easy to spend a disproportionate amount of time on the site. If you do decide to use Pinterest, will power may be required to step away and focus on the other core elements of job seeking.

Instagram

In a nutshell Instagram is a photo-sharing site where you can share photos through your own profile, as well as follow other people's accounts to see what images they are sharing.

What you can post Instagram is all about sharing images, primarily photographs. You can also share images you have found online on websites, blogs or anywhere else. It's become (in)famous for people sharing images of their dinner, but you can post images of all kinds of things that you come across and find interesting – the only limit is your own creativity. Instagram offers a range of filters, so you can edit your photographs to make them more visually appealing. You can also interact with other people on the site by liking or commenting on the images they upload.

How it can help you get a job Similarly to Pinterest, Instagram is unlikely to lead to a job by itself. What it can do is provide a great outlet for you to showcase your creative side. It is particularly useful if you are angling for a job in a creative industry, as it can serve as your online portfolio and a showcase of your particular aesthetic. Instagram can provide a less formal insight into your personality. This is important because employers like to know what kind of person you are in order to assess how well you would fit in with their company culture. A growing number of employers are using Instagram in their branding and recruitment campaigns, so this is another platform you can use to get an insight into what they value and to gather clues about how you can show that you would be a good fit.

The downside A certain amount of creativity and a moderately good eye are central to developing an engaging Instagram feed, so if you're not particularly interested in photography or don't often come across interesting things to share, this might not be the platform to use.

Choosing a platform

It's better to have one carefully managed social media profile than several competing and underused profiles. The range of options can seem overwhelming. Pick one or two social media sites to begin with, rather than overextending yourself. If you only set up one account, make it a LinkedIn account, as this is the social platform that has a professional focus. Beyond that, the choice is really yours, based on which option you find the most interesting and the one that gives you the best platform for what you want to do.

Social media is currently dominated by the big names like Facebook, Twitter, LinkedIn, Instagram and so on. It's an ever-changing space, and new platforms emerge all the time, so whenever you come across a new one and find yourself wondering if you should join, ask yourself the questions in the following tip box to help you decide whether you want to invest your time and effort there.

Assessing a social media site

When you encounter a new social media site, ask the following questions to determine if it could meet your needs:

- What does this site do well? What does it accomplish?
- Does it include features – video or photo sharing, or the option to post articles, share links of interest and connect with people – that will help me demonstrate my skills or career interests?
- Is it an active site? Will the people who matter find me here?
- Do I have the time to dedicate to using it properly?
- Are there other sites that do the same thing, only better?

There's nobody from my sector on social media...

This is a common misconception. With so many celebrities using Twitter, it can seem like it's only the preserve of famous people and fluff. In reality, there are professionals from all sectors busily tweeting about their jobs, thoughts and activities every day, from international development professionals to people running tech start-ups, and everyone in between.

LinkedIn tends to be seen as a place for CEOs and professionals from more "traditional" businesses, but the profile of members is much more diverse than that – people at all career stages, and in countless professions, who have profiles bursting with information about what they do and how they got to where they are today. You'll find everyone from computer programmers to geophysicists to priests on LinkedIn.

As for blogs, there are millions of them. Many of the most successful ones are run by people who are highly regarded in their area, from engineers to interior designers to investment bankers. You get the idea. There are definitely people from your sector of interest on social media. You just need to take a look around to find them.

Which platforms for which sectors?

LinkedIn is the leading professional networking site and the most obvious place to start when looking to leverage social media in your job search. However, all the other channels provide interesting ways to show your interests and skills, no matter what sector you want to join. The more image-based platforms like Pinterest and Instagram are particularly suitable for those with an interest in careers that involve working with interesting subjects for photography, whether that's architecture or zoology, but there are ways of using each channel for any career interest. Here are some ideas on how you can use the various channels for different types of work.

Journalism and writing Set up a blog and post your writing on it regularly. Aspiring writers need to have a portfolio of written work to show potential employers, so a blog is a simple way of centralising all your work. Use Twitter to share your blog posts, share links to the work of writers you admire and post interesting quotes you come across in your course. Set up Pinterest boards according to your different areas of interest – politics, creative writing, author inspiration – and pin interesting articles to each.

Finance Follow finance firms on Facebook, Twitter and LinkedIn. Use LinkedIn to identify a graduate from your course who is working in one of your target firms, and ask this person to connect with you and share her insight into what the firm looks for in their graduate hires. Create a blog commenting on market trends or giving advice on investing for people from a non-finance background.

Health and nutrition Use Instagram to post photographs of healthy meals you've prepared or to share images of good form for exercises. Write a blog about the interesting things you are learning throughout your course. Engage with others in this area who are active on Twitter.

Chapter 1

Arts and culture Visit museums and historical locations, and share photographs on Instagram. Link this to your Facebook account so they are posted there too. Write a blog about all the places you visit and their meaning to you. Follow the pages of artists you like on Facebook, and the company pages of cultural institutions on LinkedIn.

Not for profit Use Facebook and Twitter to promote a fundraising event you are running to raise money for a charity you support. Join groups on LinkedIn for people working in the sector, and find out what the hot topics in the sector are currently.

Science Blog about interesting new discoveries and research reports in your area of interest. Share photographs of your lab work on Instagram. Use LinkedIn to explore the career paths of other research scientists, and find out what steps you need to take to reach a similar position.

These are just a few ideas to show how versatile social media is and how it can be useful no matter what type of career you are considering.

Social media aggregators

If you do decide to set up and manage multiple profiles, social media aggregators make it easier to keep on top of everything that is happening across your accounts. Social media aggregators are sites that bring all your social media platforms together onto one page. Instead of having to open multiple tabs and needing to remember to check all your different profiles, you can simply log into whichever aggregator you choose and see all the updates in your network in one place.

There are numerous aggregators to choose from, but Hootsuite is probably the biggest name in social media management tools. You can create an account, input the details of your different social media profiles and choose which ones you want to see on your Hootsuite home screen. You can also post to one or all of your accounts directly from the landing page, and what makes this site particularly useful is the ability to schedule updates. For example, you might be up late one night reading articles online, but it might look a bit sad to be tweeting a link to a blog post about a new development in renewable energy at 2 a.m. on a Saturday night. You could log into Hootsuite, draft the post you want to share and schedule it to be posted at a more suitable time.

Scheduling posts is also useful because you might spend a few hours one day reading lots of interesting posts, blogs and articles which you'd like to share online. However, you don't want to flood people's feeds with five updates in an hour and then share nothing for weeks. By scheduling posts, you can create a steady stream of regular updates which will keep you on your network's radar on a more regular basis.

If you're keen to get your profiles and updates seen by as many people as possible, you should schedule your posts at times when they are most likely to be noticed. Research carried out to figure out the optimum time to share content on Facebook, Twitter and LinkedIn is outlined in the following table.

Best and worst times to post on Facebook, Twitter and LinkedIn			
	Facebook	Twitter	LinkedIn
Best time to post	1–4 p.m.	Mon–Thurs, 1 p.m.–3 p.m.	Tues–Thurs
Peak time	Wed 3 p.m.	Mon–Thurs 9 a.m–3 p.m.	Midday and 5 p.m.–6 p.m.
Worst time	Weekends before 8 a.m. after 8 p.m.	Every day after 8 p.m. Fri after 3 p.m.	Mon and Fri 10 p.m.–6 a.m.

Source: www.blog.surepayroll.com

Are employers really looking?

Recruiters are busy, and not every employer has the time to research candidates online. However, an increasing number of companies are looking up candidates on the Internet. This can happen at various stages in the recruitment process. It's time-consuming, so interviewers are more likely to run an online search for you in the later stages, when they have a short-list for interviews – or even after the interviews have been conducted. Larger organisations with healthy hiring budgets can buy software that pools all of the information available about you on social networks into one place. This saves time and makes it easier for them to accurately assess your online presence. If one of those companies happens to be a company you'd like to work for, assume they're looking you up online.

Employer's view: Elizabeth Murphy,

HR and Recruitment, Mobile Travel Technologies

Your social media "persona" really matters. Graduate recruiters do look at it, so start building your brand early. Have something intelligent to add to the conversation – comment on areas relevant to the career you want, join specific interest groups, follow industry leaders, etc.

I recall checking out a potential graduate's online profile, just to get a sense of where his passion/interests lay in terms of the role. His Facebook showed numerous images of him in various states of drunkenness and undress, and his posts constantly used lots of bad language and contained sexist comments. This was a person looking to work in Marketing, and his "personal brand" was way off.

Even if an employer doesn't look you up on social media, there's a good chance your new colleagues might. You'll want to make a good impression when you start at a new workplace, but if one of your new colleagues finds some of your digital dirt, it could significantly undermine your position there from the very beginning. The table on the next page outlines the main social media factors that influence employers' decisions to reject or hire candidates.

It's worth expanding on the point in the table stating that poor communication skills online can create a negative impression. Your posts should always use correct grammar, and make sure not to post anything containing spelling mistakes. Avoid text speak and overusing emoticons, as these can make you appear immature, which is the opposite of what employers want to see. It's also best to keep your language clean, so avoid swearing.

Many platforms don't have a built-in spelling and grammar checker. Where spell-check does exist, don't rely exclusively only on this. You may have included words that are correct, but not in the context in which you've used them. Be particularly careful when posting from your smartphone: autocorrect can do terrible things to innocent messages. If you're not confident in your spelling or use of grammar, you could ask a friend to review updates before you

Top social media factors impacting on your employment prospects

Top social media blunders that negatively impact on your employment prospects

- Provocative/inappropriate photos or information
- Information about you drinking or using drugs
- Bad-mouthing a previous employer
- Displaying poor communication skills
- Discriminatory comments related to race, gender, religion, etc.
- Lying about qualifications

Top social media factors that can positively influence hiring decisions

- Conveying a professional image
- Giving employers a good feel for your personality
- Showing that your are well-rounded, with a wide range of interests
- Providing background information that supports your claims about your professional qualifications
- Displaying creativity
- Demonstrating evidence of great communication skills
- Including other people's postings of great references

Source: www.careerbuilder.com.

Chapter 1

post. In any case, it's a good idea to always reread anything before clicking "post".

What to do next

Now that you know why social media should be a part of your job search strategy, head to Chapter 2 to do some ground work before you launch into setting up and managing your social networks.

Useful websites

www.tweetdeck.twitter.com and **www.netvibes.com**
These are two other free social media aggregators worth
looking into.

www.theundercoverrecruiter.com This is a very popular
blog which frequently shares posts with advice on using social
media in your job search.

www.theguardian.com The Guardian's Careers pages are a
great resource for anyone searching for work, and they have
plenty of social media resources too.

Define your brand

Contents

First things first – the idea of "branding" yourself may seem unpleasant. You're a living, breathing person, not a carton of milk or a shiny new car. "Branding" is just one of a number of marketing terms, more commonly applied to products, which pepper the world of business recruitment. It's all about "selling yourself", "identifying your market", "promoting your brand" and "knowing your USPs (unique selling points)".

These concepts can seem cold and impersonal when applied to people. However, you need to try to cast aside negative associations with these words; they are simply terms to help you think of yourself as someone who has something to offer. As a jobseeker, your current job is to present what you have to offer clearly and coherently online.

What's my brand?

Your brand is the overall impression that others have of who you are and what you can do. Managing your online footprint in a manner that highlights your experience and professional aspirations can improve your job-seeking prospects by showing employers that you're serious about your career.

Most people, at all career stages, find it hard to define who they are and what they have to offer. You may feel that you don't have a lot to show an employer at this stage. Many students and recent graduates feel that way, believing they "only" have a degree or "only" have volunteering experience. Having a degree equips you with so many more skills than you might realise. You have probably developed the ability to work on group projects, deliver presentations, manage competing coursework and make difficult decisions. If you've undertaken anything outside of your coursework, like doing part-time work, playing for a sports club or being involved in volunteering, you have also demonstrated maturity, commitment and drive.

Before you can go about effectively presenting who you are online, you need a clear understanding of what you have to offer and what you would like to do. Your brand is a mix of four key elements: your values, your interests, your personality and your skills. The groundwork involved in identifying each of these elements is probably the most time-consuming part of getting the most out of social media in your job search. Once you have a clear sense of what you want to say, it becomes much easier to decide what to write in your profiles and what to post to fit with that core brand.

Your career focus

I don't know what I want to do

Some students and graduates have a very clear idea about the exact job they would like to do. Some have an idea about the industry they want to work in and the kind of career path that they would like to follow. Many, many other students are not sure what job they want to do after their studies. If you're overcome with dread when asked the inevitable question "What are you going to do after university?", rest assured that you're not alone.

There are many tools and resources which can help you to develop a clearer sense of where your next step in the world of work should be. In addition to these, your careers service is there to help you if you're feeling lost, and even if you've already graduated, you'll find that most services will also offer support for a while afterwards.

You can help yourself to get a clearer idea of what career you might like by identifying what it is that makes you different. Once you know your personality, your skills, your interests and your values, you will get a clearer picture of how you are different to those around you and what types of careers would best fit your unique characteristics. The sections that follow will help you with this process.

I want to do several things

When you have a range of career interests, it can be challenging to know how to present yourself online. The question of how to balance your online profiles to show your various interests and experience, while not deterring people who may feel you lack focus, has no easy answer. When you're describing your skills and experience, try to give equal weight to the different things you've done so that the focus isn't so heavily weighted in one direction that employers will think you're only interested in one type of role.

Place the focus on your transferable skills and experience – achievements in any area of college, work or extracurricular activities are interesting to employers. Showcase your contributions to different teams or projects and the impact you had in different roles. Create an overall impression of somebody who is proactive and driven, and who makes a positive contribution in a range of contexts.

What you have to offer

If you were asked to make a list of everything you want to do and everything you're good at, you might find it incredibly difficult. You might find it equally challenging to define your personality and what type of job would best suit you. The resources in the following section will help you to clarify who you are, gain a clearer sense of the types of careers that interest you and identify what you have to offer an employer. They will also expand your career-related vocabulary and help you to identify what it is that makes you different; in other words, they will give you the building blocks upon which to build your brand.

Your values

Values might not seem like an obvious place to start when trying to pin down a clear picture of yourself in a career context, but they're a key component of career planning. Your career-related values specifically reflect what is important for you to achieve job satisfaction. These values can range from financial stability to wanting to be an expert in your field, from liking a job with lots of variety that really challenges you to enjoying a job with a more measured pace that allows you time to delve in depth into longer-term projects.

A quick way of defining your work values is to use a values card sort tool. You can find the Knowdell Career Values card sort free online at http://stewartcoopercoon.com. This exercise only takes about five minutes, but it's extremely useful. Knowing your career values is a core part of helping you to complete your career direction puzzle.

Exercise: List the top six values that stood out for you after completing the values assessment	
Your core career values	
1.	4.
2.	5.
3.	6.

Where your values align with the work environment in a company you want to join and with the requirements of the role you're interested in, they are a real asset to you, and therefore to the company. Having clarity about what matters to you in a job will also help you to create a more convincing argument as to why you would be a great fit for specific roles.

Your personality

Your personality plays an important role in your career choice. The type of person you are has a significant impact on your career happiness. To give you a sense of why personality matters, take the example of one often-discussed aspect of personality, extraversion, and it's opposite, introversion. In reality these are not true opposites; extraversion and introversion are at either end of a graduated scale. You might be very much an extrovert, very much an introvert or somewhere in between the two.

If you're more extroverted, you get your energy from being around others, and you would thrive in a job where you're interacting with

Chapter 2

people a lot in your day-to-day work. You would likely feel drained
and unhappy in a role which requires a lot of solitary work. If you tend
to be more introverted, you'll prefer work where you can spend large
portions of time by yourself, and you would likely be much happier
working in a quiet environment.

The introversion–extraversion scale is only one facet of personality.
There are several others to consider, and when these are all taken
together, they can provide key indicators as to the type of career
where you would be at your best. The personality self-assessment
available for free at http://www.findingpotential.com is a useful online
psychometric test which asks you to answer a series of questions about
your preferences. This assessment will generate a detailed report that
shows you what kind of tasks you would likely prefer as a core part of
your working life. It is invaluable information for anybody considering
career options. Knowing what environments and tasks are best suited
to your personality will help you to assess job types according to how
well they fit your profile.

Self-assessment: Your personality

Complete the personality questionnaire on finding potential. Note
the personality and circle the number that indicates where your
personality fits along each of the five personality scales.

Extraversion	1 2 3 4 5 6 7 8 9 10
Openness	1 2 3 4 5 6 7 8 9 10
Agreeableness	1 2 3 4 5 6 7 8 9 10
Conscientiousness	1 2 3 4 5 6 7 8 9 10
Resilience	1 2 3 4 5 6 7 8 9 10

Your personality is part of what you have to offer to an employer. If
you are applying for a role that is highly stressful, for example as an
investment analyst or a role in a busy law firm, having a high level
of resilience will help you to succeed. If you are very conscientious,
this trait will be very valuable in roles that require discretion and
adherence to strict protocols. And if you are introverted, your ability

to focus on and manage your work independently will be valuable in a role that requires these skills. You will do your best work in a role that fits with your personality and in an environment that suits you well. If you can let your personality come through in your online profiles and you can identify the ways in which your personality is an advantage in a job, it will help you to succeed in the hiring process.

Your interests

Interest inventories can help you narrow down your interests and get a clear picture of the type of jobs which you would find engaging. It's likely that many of your interests fall within a small number of categories. Although it's impossible to get an exhaustive list of all jobs related to specific interests, as existing careers go out of fashion and new jobs emerge all the time, knowing the broad areas that appeal to you is a good starting point. You might tend more towards jobs that are very practical, or you might be more interested in creative roles or roles that involve working with data, for example. To help you develop a good understanding of your interests, try the O*NET Interest Profiler, which you can find at http://www.mynextmove.org/explore/ip. It will take you approximately 20 minutes to answer around 60 questions, after which you will be given a list of your top interests.

Self-assessment: Your interests

Complete the interest assessment, and write down the two career categories that are most of interest to you. Beside this, list two jobs within each category that could be of interest to you.

Interest category	Related roles
A	1. 2.
B	1. 2.

Don't underestimate how much your real interest in a job or industry can help you in your job search. There are so many applicants for every job, and you can stand out by showing employers that you genuinely want to build a career in their sector. In a situation where you are competing with other graduates with similar skills for the same job, this will set you apart. Social media provides many ways for you to provide evidence that you want to do the type of work you say you want to do, so use it to your advantage.

Your skills

You will have developed a range of skills and abilities through your studies and part-time work, volunteering and membership of extracurricular groups, and participation in activities outside of your courses. You may feel that you don't have many skills by the time you graduate, but in reality you'd have to make a very concerted effort to get through an entire university course without developing a single skill. It's very useful to do a skills inventory to help you recognise everything you can already do.

You'll find a skills inventory at www.iseek.org/careers/skillsAssessment. It will present you with a list of statements about yourself. Go through the list and tick any that apply to you. By the end of the inventory, you'll find that you have many more skills than you realised.

Chapter 2

Self-assessment: Your skills
Once you've completed the skills inventory, list four key skills you identified in the table below.
Key skills
1.
2.
3.
4.

Skills from experience

The skills inventory is a quick way to gain a general sense of your skills. To make your skills meaningful, you need to identify where you have demonstrated those skills. Every activity you participate in adds to your skill set and helps you to discover your expertise. Even if you "only" studied for the duration of your degree, you will have developed time management, research and writing skills, and many more that will help you become an asset to your employer.

The more activities you've been in involved in, the more opportunities you'll have had to improve your skill set. If you're reading this book early in your college course, it would be wise to get involved in something outside of your coursework as soon as possible. Employers frequently state that they would rather hire somebody with a 2.1 overall grade and lots of real-world experience than somebody with a first class honours degree who spent four years in a library and doesn't have as much practical experience.

To identify your skills, you need to review all of your involvement in, and contribution to, activities, projects, groups and teams over the past few years. This will provide you with the evidence you need to back up the claims you make when you apply for work. The next exercise will get you thinking specifically about what you have to offer.

Making the connection

Now that you have a clear picture of your skills, the next step is to start linking them to jobs. Job descriptions usually include a list of core skills that the employer is looking for in a candidate. These will include specific skills, such as being able to use particular software, speaking a second language, being able to draft architectural plans and so on. The other category of skills that are usually listed are transferable, or "soft" skills. These include things like these:

- Communication
- Interpersonal skills
- Time management
- Project management
- Teamwork
- Leadership.

Exercise: Your skills in action

There are four experience categories listed in the boxes below. For each category, list one specific activity in which you took part and the skills you gained or improved upon while doing so. Once you've filled this out, you should have a much better idea of the very real skills you have to offer.

Activity	Skills demonstrated
Volunteering	
Coursework	
Part-time work	
Extracurricular activity – sport, drama, etc.	

All too often, students overlook the importance of these skills. Somebody in Human Resources has taken the time to write the job description and define the transferable skills necessary for the job, so ignore them at your peril. By now you should have a clear sense of some of your strongest skills. You need to pay attention to the transferable skills that employers have outlined as advantageous, and then you should determine how to describe yourself in a job application or in online profiles so that you can demonstrate that you have these abilities.

The keys to the kingdom

When you are faced with the challenge of convincing an employer that you match the requirements for the job, skills are only one part of the equation. Keywords are equally important. Keywords are specific words relating to different aspects of a job description. They can refer to a variety of different concepts such as specific skills, knowledge, attributes, interests and attitudes. Identifying keywords related to the job you want to do is an essential part of making yourself stand out from other graduates. When you know what keywords are essential in the job you want, you can incorporate these into your social media profiles and posts to make your brand align with employer expectations.

Getting your keywords right is essential for your CV too, particularly if you're planning on applying to a large corporation. Many companies use applicant tracking systems that scan your applications for keywords, so if you don't include the right ones, a machine could reject your application before a human ever gets to see it. Therefore, this work on keywords will help you in all areas of your search, on and offline.

Find your keys

Finding keywords takes a little bit of legwork. Read through job descriptions you are interested in, paying attention to the words used to describe the role and the ideal candidate. This sample job description has the keywords highlighted to show you how.

Chapter 2

Sample job description with keywords

Pharmaceutical Sales Representative
The applicant will work with a sales manager to **research market trends** and follow up with **market research** on specific territories. The applicant will **represent the company** and any **products** assigned to a specific territory, and the representative must promote the company as needed.

Applicant must **offer accurate information** to **healthcare personnel** so that products will be understood and used correctly. Applicant must exhibit high **performance** and **leadership** capabilities and be **confident working independently** with minimal supervision in the field.

Necessary skills and experience:
- **Sales Experience**
- Track record of working successfully to **targets**
- Knowledge **of pharmaceutical products**
- The ability to **understand and convey complex information**
- **Market research** skills
- Excellent **interpersonal communication** skills
- A **Bachelor's Degree** or higher with preferred areas of study including **pharmacy, sciences** or **healthcare**

This job description should give you a really good sense of how to identify keywords. Here is another example for you to use to identify the key terms.

Exercise: Identify keywords

Read the job description below, and circle the keywords. Answers are listed at the end of the description.

Graduate financial analyst
We are hiring graduate financial analysts to support the operation and implementation of automated trading strategies. The successful candidate will work closely with Traders on the trading desks to monitor risk and verify trading activity. We are looking for someone with a strong understanding of information technology who can demonstrate consistently strong academic achievement. If you meet our requirements and are interested in starting a career in finance, we would like to hear from you.

- A third-level quantitative degree in maths, physics or a related field
- An excellent understanding of electronic markets
- Proficiency in Excel and VBA and some programming experience
- Excellent problem-solving skills

Keywords in this job description include:

financial analyst, operations, implementation, automated trading strategies, traders, monitor risk, verify, trading activity, information technology, academic achievement, finance, quantitative, maths, physics, electronic markets, Excel, VBA, programming, problem-solving.

Are you starting to notice keywords in these job descriptions? As you go through descriptions of jobs you want, you can start to pick out the keywords that you will need to include in your own applications and online profiles. Do the following exercise to practise this on a live job description.

Chapter 2

Exercise: Identify your keywords

Find a vacancy online; you'll find these on a jobs board on your university careers website. Click into a job description, and read it carefully to understand what the employer is looking for. Pick out six keywords you would need to include in your online profile or application if you were interested in applying for this role, and list them in the boxes below.

1.	2.	3.
4.	5.	6.

This is definitely not rocket science, but it works. Once you can train yourself to read job descriptions for keywords, you'll find that everything, from drafting your online profiles and posts to tailoring your CV and preparing great interview answers, becomes much easier.

Putting it all together

Look back over all the exercises that you have completed in this chapter. You should now have a clear list of your personality traits, interests, values and demonstrated skills. Together, these are what make you unique as a candidate. This is what you want to put across to employers. Your brand, in other words, is a combination of all your traits, interests and experience.

Use the following table to gather your findings in one place. This will make it easier for you to create and build your social media profiles and to focus your updates online.

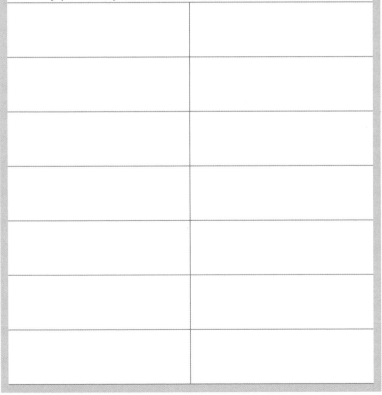

Exercise: Your brand

Go back through all the exercises you have completed in this chapter. Gather all the key personality traits, interests, career values, skills and keywords related to specific careers that you have identified, and list them in the table below.

Your key personality, skills, values and interests	

Your career keywords	

What to do next

Now that you know what you have to offer, and what you want employers to know about you, head to Chapter 3 to find out how to use all the work you've done to make your online presence reflect how employable you are. There are a lot of different elements to go through in this chapter, so if you're not feeling completely clear about what you have learned thus far, go back over any exercises you feel you need to spend more time on. If you understand what you want your online brand to be, read the next few chapters to see how to take these ideas and put them into action on social media.

Chapter 2

Put your brand online

Contents

- Assess what's out there
- Clean up your past
- Dealing with discrimination
- Put your brand online
- Consistency is key
- Your social calendar
- No negativity
- What to do next
- Useful websites

Whether you already have a profile or two, or you're just getting started on social media, you need to think about the impression you are giving through your online presence. This chapter will take you through the key steps to making sure you're presenting yourself online in a way that helps – rather than hinders – your efforts in finding a job. Start by reviewing what's already out there and then get to work managing your online presence.

Assess what's out there

You may already have social media profiles, but it's possible you haven't taken them too seriously up until this point. It's time to make some changes. Your potential employers could look at your entire online presence, and this includes all your social media profiles. The quickest way to know what your digital footprint looks like right now is to put your name into a search engine and see what comes up. Most people don't look beyond the first page or so of search results, but if someone is very interested in finding out more about you, they may search a little further. So, carry out a search for your name and check the first three to four pages to see what's there. Look at the image search results as well. Take stock of the information available online about you. If potential employers were looking at these search results right now, what would they think? Would the information they've found make them more likely to hire you, or less likely? Would they find very little and be left with not much of an impression of you at all?

You should evaluate any and all social media accounts you currently have to assess the image you're portraying. Do the following exercise to review one of your profiles, and reflect on what message you are currently sending out online.

Exercise: What message am I sending?

Pick an existing social media profile you own, if you have one. Ask yourself the following questions, and jot down your impressions in the space provided.

Have I made my career interests clear on this profile in the last three months? Circle as appropriate.

Yes, consistently   **Yes, once or twice**   **Not at all**

If someone looked at this account, what general impression would he or she have of me? List the three words that spring to mind as you review your profile.

1.

2.

3.

Carry out this exercise while looking at each of your profiles individually. Once you have a clear sense of what your current online image is, it will make it easier for you plan how to make it work for you from here on in.

Clean up your past

Every social media platform has privacy settings. These allow you to control how much you share through your profile. This can range from sharing no information with the public, which might be a good idea for your Facebook profile, to letting everyone see what you post, which works well with sites like Twitter and LinkedIn once you're using them correctly – and you will be by the time you reach the end of this book.

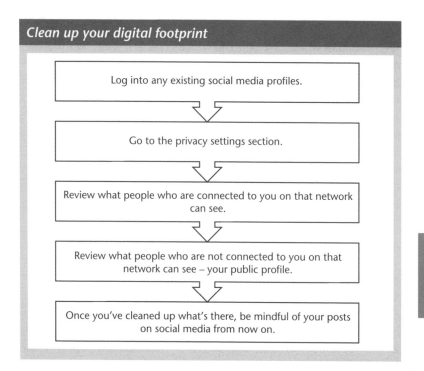

Clean up your digital footprint

Log into any existing social media profiles.

Go to the privacy settings section.

Review what people who are connected to you on that network can see.

Review what people who are not connected to you on that network can see – your public profile.

Once you've cleaned up what's there, be mindful of your posts on social media from now on.

Check the privacy settings on any and all social media accounts you already have. Take a look at the settings on your Facebook posts as well as your photo albums. If you have a public Twitter feed, scroll through your tweets, and delete anything that could be viewed as offensive or inappropriate. If you blog or comment on other blogs, scan what you've written online, and delete anything that might go against you. This includes photos or posts that portray you as a party animal, and any negative or discriminatory comments. Deleting this type of post is damage control, and it's the absolute minimum that you should to if you're serious about finding a job.

Spending time going back over your old posts is admittedly not a fun way to spend a few hours, but it's worth doing. Once you have done everything within your control to prevent any existing online information standing in the way of your successful job search, you can focus on making social media work for you in a proactive way. The aim is to let any hiring managers who look into your background know that you are the employee they want. The next few chapters will show you how to do just that.

An online tool which can help you with all of this is www.reppler.com. It's a social media monitoring site where you can set up an account by logging in with various social media accounts, including Twitter, LinkedIn and Facebook. Once you connect your accounts to Reppler, it scans your existing profiles for tone and content, and alerts you to any posts it identifies as being inappropriate or negative. It will provide a direct link to anything it assesses as requiring attention, making it easy for you to delete any damaging updates or photographs. It's not foolproof, and you shouldn't rely only on it, but it can certainly speed up the process of reviewing what you already have online and removing posts that could work against you.

Advising you to be aware of all of your online interactions may seem excessive, but it's human nature to be curious. At one time or another, everyone has ended up in Internet black holes, clicking through completely random information based on what comes up on a website. One minute you're checking your Facebook timeline. The next you're clicking through your friend's cousin's holiday photos. The idea is not to become paranoid, but simply to be mindful about what you post, while exercising common sense.

You can't change the past, but you can control what you share online from here onwards. Post with the knowledge that everything you share online could potentially be there forever. Be conscious of what you post on every site, and be aware of the content other people post about you online. If friends have shared questionable photographs or anecdotes online in which you are tagged or mentioned, untag yourself, or ask if they could remove them.

Damage control

It can be difficult to maintain a completely clean slate online. You can control your own posts, but you have less control over what other people post and share about you. From college parties to blog rants to shared Facebook posts to Vine® videos, your private life can often slip into the public eye, and this could tarnish the online brand you're going to be working to create. There are several steps you can take to make sure you are putting your best digital foot forward and to minimise the impact of anything potentially damaging.

Be prepared Know what your online "blemishes" – if any – could be, and prepare explanations if they happen to come up in an interview. Don't make excuses; what happened, happened. Offer brief, reasonable explanations, and move on to talk about more positive work you've done since then. As an example, if you are in an interview and the interviewer says that she looked you up online and mentions that she came across quite a few photographs of you out partying, don't just sit there blushing and mumbling: address it head-on. Explain that the photographs are on the Facebook page of a friend and that you asked the friend to remove them but he hasn't done so yet. Acknowledge that you realise this doesn't create the best impression but that you hope she will see past that and understand that, although you let your hair down outside of work, you are serious and committed when it comes to the workplace. You could conclude with a positive angle by pointing to your achievements which prove this, in an explanatory rather than a defensive manner.

Shift the focus Although past indiscretions (if they exist) can't always be scrubbed entirely, the best way to negate them is to present an otherwise strong online brand that plays to your strengths and recent accomplishments. Having multiple social media channels can prove helpful. Between LinkedIn, Twitter, Instagram and individual blog posts, you can create enough career-focused, employment-enhancing content to hopefully push less favourable content further down in the search results.

Your right to be forgotten The "right to be forgotten" ruling in effect in Europe enables you to request that Google® stop certain search results from appearing when specific terms are entered into the search engine. Whenever Google agrees that it is not in the public interest for these links to be searchable, the company can execute this request. This only applies to European Union (EU) versions of Google and not to web searches done on google.com, whether you are searching from a computer within the EU or outside the EU. Although this means that search results will not lead directly to particular pages, the pages themselves will still be available online.

Chapter 3

This is not a mechanism which can wipe the Internet clean of everything you would like to erase; it simply makes certain pages harder to find. A particularly interested person, including your potential employer, could still locate these pages through other means. This isn't the forum to deal with the rights and wrongs of this facility, and it's up to you to choose to use it, if it applies where you live. If there's something incriminating about you available online, it might be worth investigating whether this option is open to you.

Apply to be forgotten

Is there something online that could affect your job prospects that you would like to have removed from Google search results? Depending on your location and other criteria, the "right to be forgotten" legislation could work in your favour. You can find the removal request form on https://support.google.com.

Dealing with discrimination

Depending on where you live, there can often be legislation in place that attempts to prevent discrimination in the hiring process. There's no doubt that it is morally – and very often legally – wrong for employers to discriminate against candidates. Despite this, discrimination can, unfortunately, still occur. You might be concerned that the information available about you online could unfairly, and often illegally, hamper your employment prospects. Your likes, dislikes, pictures, profiles, videos and affiliations are all online for anyone to find in one quick search. Such a wealth of information makes it easier

---

Factors for which people can experience discrimination include:

- Political beliefs
- Race
- Sexual orientation
- Disability
- Marital status
- Religious affiliation
- Gender
- Socio-economic background
- University attended
- Age

than ever for companies to discriminate against you, based not only on how you look but also according to who you are, what you believe and where you come from.

As a student or graduate in the early stages of your career, you'll likely want to draw upon all of the different experiences you've had to date in order to fully highlight your skills and abilities. Sometimes, this experience might come under a category that could potentially lead to discrimination, such as the following:

● Your active role in the campus LGBT society
● Your work as a campaign assistant to a politician
● Your role as a youth leader within a religious organisation
● Your involvement in campaigning for citizens' rights
● A fundraising activity you carried out to support a mental health charity that helped you through your own mental health issue.

These are just a few examples of activities in which you may have taken part. In each, you will likely have displayed skills and attributes which provide important evidence to employers about the talent you could bring to their organisation. In addition, being involved in employment and volunteer activities which go beyond your coursework shows dedication and commitment – two attractive attributes of a great employee. You should be proud of all your experience and achievements, and the best way to demonstrate your skills is to provide clear, achievement-focused evidence of all that you have done in your CV, on LinkedIn and on any other appropriate platform. It would be a real shame to miss out on the opportunity to describe these experiences, particularly if you have little other practical experience to draw upon in order to showcase your potential.

This raises the issue of how to balance the desire to highlight your background with the fact that you don't want to be discriminated against in your job search. If there is something that you are particularly worried about, and you feel like you really do want to try to keep something out of the limelight, then there are ways of reframing your experience to minimise the risk of discrimination.

Reframe your experience

Your goal as a jobseeker is to find employment, and you need to gather together as much evidence as possible to show that you are up to the task. If you have enough experience to write about in your application and talk about in your interview, you might be able to leave out anything which you feel might leave you open to discrimination. Note that this is a risky strategy as it removes the possibility of explaining the breadth of your experience, and might even leave your profile somewhat bland, with little to differentiate it from that of other candidates.

The other option would be to be creative with how you write about your experience. There are lots of ways to write about this. If you are applying for a leadership role and your best example of past leadership is working as a youth group leader for your local church, and you're concerned that an employer might discriminate against you based on your religious affiliation, you could list this as: "Youth Leader – Local Community Group". This becomes a way of using the experience without drawing attention to your religious affiliation. Doing this is not always simple, but a little creativity can go a long way.

Proceed with caution when seeking to reduce potential discrimination. The different activities in which you are involved all contribute to making you a unique and interesting person to work with. There can be a tendency to assume the worst: that employers are narrow-minded and might only employ candidates from a very specific racial, gender, religious or geographical demographic. The fact is, employers are as diverse as the general population, and the thing you might want to hide could actually make your application stand out in a positive way, leading to you being shortlisted for the exact job you want.

Put your brand online

Social and personal

Now that you've done all you can to ensure that what's already out there about you is not going to get in your way, it's time to work on getting the message out about what you have to offer. Imagine how impactful it would be if a potential employer were to look you up online and find a steady feed of thoughtful articles you've written or shared from industry websites and blogs; interactions with thought leaders in your industry; and pictures, videos and links about recent industry developments. Now compare that experience to someone coming across an uncensored feed full of comments about skipping lectures or missing deadlines, reposted memes and photos of endless nights out. There's no comparison.

Your personality It's the "social" in "social media" that comes first. Brands are personal – or at least they should be. Presenting a rigidly career-focused profile might show that you're serious about your next step, but you should try to let employers get to know your personality a little through your profiles. Nobody wants to hire a robot. Employers pay a lot of attention to the "cultural fit" of candidates; in other words they want to know if your personality will fit in well with their ethos and existing team. Letting your personality shine through in your social media profiles can help employers to assess this fit even before they meet you in person.

This doesn't mean you need to give a blow-by-blow account of your life in constant Twitter updates, or post every picture of every meal you eat on Instagram – unless you're aiming for a career as a chef. Feel free to be yourself, and share snapshots of your life interspersed with career-related content. If you're competing against several candidates with qualifications broadly similar to your own, it might be the photos you share of yourself doing a charity run or taking part in a debate competition that cause you to catch the eye of an employer.

Your interests Sharing a mixture of great content by others, alongside your own thoughts, photographs or blog posts, will show your online network where your interests lie. For example, if you're aiming for a career in photography, build a website to showcase your work, and use other platforms to like and share pages, posts, graphics and videos that reflect your aesthetic. Or if you're interested in a career in software development, create a blog to showcase any projects you have worked on, and share articles about other people's work that you find interesting in relevant LinkedIn groups or on your Twitter feed.

Your values Your values can be quite tied to your personality traits, and you can showcase them in a similar way. For example, if you are someone who strongly values teamwork, make sure to highlight your work with teams in your LinkedIn profile, or tweet about group activities you've really enjoyed. If you're engaged in any sport or volunteering with a team, you could share photographs from work that you do which feature the team you work with. If you're someone who values making a difference in society, post updates about causes

Chapter 3

that interest you, and follow and interact with organisations that have a social mission, or share links to the corporate social responsibility initiatives of companies you want to join.

Employer's view: Sinéad D'Arcy, Jameson Graduate Programme Manager, Irish Distillers Pernod Ricard

In an increasingly competitive employment environment, it is becoming ever more important to build a professional online presence. Social media offers the perfect platform to build brand *YOU*. This could be as simple as demonstrating you are an enthusiastic graduate or showcasing key employability skills such as creativity, innovation and leadership.

There are lots of social media platforms available; each has its strengths and weaknesses when it comes to building a personal brand. It's vitally important to be conscious of the line between personal and professional social media engagement, so why not start thinking like a recruiter by reviewing your current social media footprint, reviewing your privacy settings and selecting your employment Social Media Mix.

As an employer, my advice to graduates would be to take the time to plan what you are going to incorporate on your social media profiles, from photos through to keywords. As with any online channel, content is king, and this content should be compelling and relevant. What do you want potential employers to know about you?

Social media offers great opportunities to get creative and build an online résumé using video, SlideShare® or even Pinterest. So rethink how you engage with social media and use it to your advantage to build brand *YOU* and start your career.

Your skills Your soft skills can be more challenging to highlight than some other elements of your brand. The best way to outline all of your skills is to have a detailed LinkedIn profile where you clearly highlight your skill set with evidence of where you've demonstrated these skills. If you have "hard" skills, these can be easier to showcase in different ways. If you speak a foreign language, consider creating a LinkedIn profile in your second language, blogging in a different language or creating a video CV where you speak your native tongue and your acquired language. If you are a graphic designer, make a blog where you post your design projects, and share links to any work you have done for societies, companies or friends. The list really is endless, so now that you know your skills, you need to give serious thought not only to outlining them but to demonstrating them online where possible.

Your keywords The easiest way to include your keywords on social media is to use them in the profiles that you build. The greater the number of times you've included a keyword in your profile, the higher it will rank in search results for those terms. However, overstuffing your profiles with keywords would be a bad idea too. Don't get to the point where you are including so many keywords that sentences lose their meaning. This is unprofessional, and it can even cause you to appear lower down within search engine rankings.

To discover the most frequently used keywords in your online profiles, simply copy all of the text in your profile and paste it into a word cloud generator. These are available for free on websites such as www.wordle.net or www.tagcloud.com, and will list words in the cloud according to how many times they are used in the text. These sites will display the words which occur most frequently in the text in a larger font size so that you have a better idea of what terms you are using the most. If the key elements that you want to highlight are not coming out strongly, you should revisit your text and find ways to use more keywords in everything you write and share.

Here are two examples of online profiles. In each bio, you will see that keywords have been marked in bold.

Example of a LinkedIn summary with keywords highlighted in bold:

I am a **graphic designer** with experience of creating **graphics** and **logos** for **web** and **print** materials. I have worked with a variety of clients including **student societies, charities** and **small to medium enterprises**, on **designs** for **flyers, online advertisements** and **websites**. I have a portfolio of work ranging from **blog design** to **brand identity** to **print** design. I would like to use my knowledge and experience to offer my **web** and **print design** skills and provide **creative** and original options to new clients.

Example of a Twitter bio:

> London-based **German** speaker, **Java** programmer, **app developer** and kite surfer.

These are just some ways you could incorporate your skills, personality, interests, values and keywords into your profiles. As you go through the chapters on individual social media sites, keep these in mind, and be conscious of coming back to all the core things you want to communicate that you have identified so far.

Consistency is key

Aim to create a coherent impression of who you are across all of your social media platforms, whether you use two or twenty. It's a good idea to cross-publicise your accounts to increase their visibility for anyone looking at you online. This kind of brand fluidity across all of your social media channels will help create the type of online presence that will give you an edge in your job search.

When you create new content on any of your social media accounts, think about posting it somewhere else also. Don't do this constantly, as the repetition can be tiresome, and different platforms require different types of content. It might make sense to link your Instagram account with your Facebook account so that any photos you share on Instagram automatically go onto your Facebook feed. It might not be appropriate to post the same content from your Twitter account on your LinkedIn account, as you might be mixing professional posts with more personal ones on Twitter, which wouldn't be appropriate on LinkedIn. The table

How to cross promote your social media profiles.	
This table outlines several ideas about how you can cross-promote your different profiles on various platforms.	
Profile	**How you can use it to share your other profiles**
Twitter	• Include your blog address, website or LinkedIn profile in your Twitter bio. • Tweet when you post something to your Pinterest board or publish a new blog post.

LinkedIn	• Include your Twitter handle in your contact details. • Mention your blog in your "Summary" section and share the link, and give it its own entry under "Experience" or list it as a project. • Post updates about new blog posts to your newsfeed.
Facebook	• List your Twitter handle, blog address or LinkedIn profile address in the "About Me" section. • Post your blog updates to your newsfeed. • Link your Instagram account to your Facebook account so your photos are automatically posted on your timeline.
Your blog	• Include contact details on the "About me" section of your blog, listing your Twitter handle or LinkedIn profile. • Write a blog post referencing an article you came across on Twitter, and embed a link to the tweet to drive readers to your account.

Chapter 3

below outlines several ideas for cross-promoting your different profiles on various platforms.

Another simple way to promote your accounts is to include links to your profiles in your email signature. Be selective here; a long list of links could seem overwhelming and prevent people from clicking at all. Also, think about which profiles would be useful to link to within your emails. For example, you should probably keep your Facebook profile out of your signature, but if you run your own business and have a Facebook page where you promote that, it might be interesting to include it. It would be reasonable to include your personalised LinkedIn URL (more on that in Chapter 6 on LinkedIn) and your Twitter handle or blog address, if either of these are appropriate to share in a professional context. Customise your email signature by stating, "Connect with me on LinkedIn www.linkedin.com/yoururl and follow me on Twitter @gradjobsearch."

Levels of engagement

You can choose to be very active on social media, and this book will give you plenty of ideas about the different ways you can harness it in your job search. On the other hand, you might prefer not to have it take up too much of your time, and you might not like the idea of regularly updating your various profiles and thinking of things to post online. You can make social media work for you without spending too much time managing your accounts. If you would prefer to keep your social media presence professional, but not time-consuming, you can certainly do this in several ways.

You could set up a great LinkedIn profile so that employers will see it when they look you up, and you could leave it at that without getting involved in groups and networking. You could set up a Twitter account and find and follow other accounts that share helpful information for your job search, and you don't have to tweet at all. Similarly you could set up a Pinterest or Instagram account and follow others, without posting anything on your own accounts. Or you could find and bookmark some useful blogs and check them regularly without commenting on posts or creating your own blog. These are just a few ways you can take advantage of all the information social media provides without having to spend too much of your time managing your profiles. It's completely up to you to decide what ways you would prefer to use it in your job search.

Your social calendar

If you decide that you want to be quite active on social media, allocate time to manage your accounts. This will help to ensure that you are not neglecting them. It also limits the amount of time you invest. Social media can become addictive, and it's easy to get sucked in and let it take up all your time. Although social media is an incredibly useful tool, there are other activities you need to spend time doing. Remember that social media can enhance your job search but doesn't remove the need for other job hunting activities, such as researching opportunities, writing your applications, conducting informational interviews and doing practice interviews to prepare you for the real thing.

Depending on which profiles you have, you may need to dedicate three hours per week to writing a weekly blog post, or 20 minutes per day if you're reviewing your Twitter feed and posting one daily tweet. A social media schedule will help you make the most of what social media has to offer without letting it become a drain on your time.

The following table will help you think about how much time you can realistically dedicate to reading updates and writing posts on one or more online profiles. In the table, indicate how much time you intend to spend every week on the following key tasks for each of your social media platforms.

Self-assessment: Your social media commitment				
	LinkedIn	Twitter	Blogging	Other platforms
Time spent reading updates	____ mins	____ mins	____ mins	____ mins
Time researching content to share/ comment on	____ mins	____ mins	____ mins	____ mins
Time spent composing your post	____ mins	____ mins	____ mins	____ mins
TOTAL	____ mins	____ mins	____ mins	____ mins

No negativity

Employers are human, and they want to hire people who are easy to work with and who will fit in well with their existing team. Avoid being overly negative in your online posts. We all have moments of frustration, and venting about them online can feel cathartic. Doing this with a sense of humour, interspersed with other more enthusiastic and engaging posts, shouldn't cause problems. However, if the predominant tone of your Twitter feed or blog is negative, you run the risk of alienating employers. Nobody wants a miserable, ranting colleague.

Never, ever post anything negative online about an employer. Other employers who see this will be concerned that you might post negatively about them, and no business wants that kind of bad publicity. If you had a terrible experience and were treated badly in an interview – and you really can't bear not sharing it online – talk about the experience, but don't mention the company. It's best to confine these posts to a Facebook profile with tight privacy settings. Even then, you run the risk that someone in your network will know somebody in the company you're talking about. Worse still, there could be somebody reading that post who works in another company you want to work for, and you could miss out on a recommendation if that person gets the impression that you're likely to share a lot of information about your boss, colleagues or company. Avoid this mistake at all costs.

What to do next

If you're not completely clear on what you want to say online, revisit Chapter 2 to gain a clear sense of your brand. If you feel ready to put this into practice, go to Chapters 6 through 9 to develop your social media profiles with your brand in mind.

Useful websites

www.careerealism.com This job site includes a blog with extensive advice on personal branding.

https://klout.com/home This website allows you to measure your impact online and gives you a score based on how much reach you have. It also helps you by providing links to articles related to your interests that you can share on your various profiles. This takes a bit of the legwork out and can be useful when you're getting started.

www.quintcareers.com This well-established site covers all the key things you need to think about in your job search, including managing your online brand.

Boost your job search

When you apply for a role, effective use of social media can provide you with a competitive advantage. Leverage social media to find out about more jobs, achieve a better understanding of what's involved in various positions, learn what makes companies unique and what they look for in candidates, make your applications stand out and ace your interviews. The amount of information you have at your fingertips can make a very real positive impact in your job search, so this chapter will take you through how you can use it to your advantage.

How businesses use social media to hire

Employers are increasingly using social media to improve their recruitment processes. They use it for three essential reasons:

1. To build their brand and engage with prospective customers and employees.
2. To research potential hires already on their radar.
3. To find great candidates to interview and hire.

Graduate employers invest a lot of time and effort into attracting, selecting and training the brightest and best because they know this will help them gain a competitive edge in their industry. Social media is being used in creative and surprising ways by all sorts of businesses, for roles at many different levels. Here are some ways that businesses have used social media in their recruitment campaigns:

> **EY** has an extensive Facebook page featuring news about the company, as well as an interactive "Global Quiz" to engage with potential hires. It also manages an active Twitter account and encourages employees to share snaps of their working life on Instagram.[4]
>
> **Mars** used a Twitter campaign to raise their brand awareness among students about their graduate recruitment campaign.[5]
>
> **Marriot Hotels, Inc.** developed an online game where users manage a virtual kitchen in order to attract more employees in the 18–27 age bracket.[6]
>
> **The US Navy** used a Facebook code-breaking game to find people with the necessary skills to become cryptologists.[7]
>
> **Starfighter,** a start-up, aims to identify candidates with a high level of programming talent. It creates complex online games which test players' abilities, and then works to place those who have demonstrated their aptitude by reaching the highest level in the game.[8]

It might seem incredibly hard to find work right now, but companies are also finding it hard to locate the right people to hire. They want graduates who are intelligent, enthusiastic and full of potential, but they also want to hire employees who are interested in their brand.

Engaging with them on social media and connecting with them across platforms can help bring you to their attention. Find and follow your target companies on Twitter, like their company page on Facebook, and follow them on LinkedIn.

Engage with employers

Go a step further by getting involved with any online games or social media campaigns they run. The more you interact with a company, the better understanding you will have of the company culture. This can help you to decide if it is the right organisation for you. It can also give you great material to draw on when you're answering questions in your applications and interviews about why you really want to work for them. Your interactions could be anything from "liking" a Facebook post to sharing one of their tweets. To get you started, complete the exercise below.

Exercise: Engaging with employers

1. Pick a company you would like to work for.
2. Visit the company web page, and go to the "Contact us" section to see what social media profiles it has.
3. Take a look at what is being shared on each profile, and list one way you could engage with the posts on each channel.

Company name: _____

Social media channel:	How I can engage with them
Social media channel:	How I can engage with them

It's easy to become enthusiastic about this approach for a couple of days and then to forget to keep track of your accounts and to interact with companies. You could incorporate interacting with companies into your social media schedule from Chapter 3, to help you remember to make this a part of your social strategy.

Social recruiting

A recent survey by the applicant-tracking-system supplier Jobvite® found that 94 per cent of companies planned to use social media in the hiring process, and about 78 per cent of companies successfully hired candidates they found through social media outlets. "Social recruiting", the term used by recruiters employing social media to unearth great candidates, is a hot topic right now. There is a very real "war for talent" going on, with companies fighting to get the best employees in order to attain a competitive edge.

It's important to be realistic about how much social media can help you "get found" at this stage. As you develop in your career, you could be headhunted by employers looking for people with a specific skill set. Right now, the chances of being plucked out of the Internet by an employer are probably slim, unless you have been particularly busy in and out of college and have already developed a niche skill set that is in demand.

At this stage in your career, it's more likely that companies will look you up once you are on their radar, perhaps when they're deciding whom to hire after they have interviewed you and are assessing your suitability. Despite this fact, it's useful to know how they do go about trying to find great candidates, and this information will become increasingly relevant in the next few years of your career. For now, it's worth thinking like a recruiter and building your profiles accordingly. The more you tailor your online content, the better impression your profiles will make on any employer who might decide to look you up online at any stage during the hiring process.

How employers find great candidates

When employers search for candidates for a specific job, they run an online search using specific keywords that are somehow connected to that role. They then search social networks to find people with those keywords in their profiles. There are a lot of prospective employees already out there with online profiles, so you will be competing with them for attention. In order for recruiters to find you, you need to be exceptionally easy to locate. Populating your social media accounts with the keywords associated with your target jobs can make you easier to find. It also means that if employers specifically look you up, they will find social media profiles that reinforce your fit with the role for which you have applied.

Boolean search terms

Recruiters use Boolean search methods to source candidates. The term "Boolean search" refers to the use of search operators like AND, NOT and OR to uncover search results that meet specific criteria. This simple approach is the way social recruiters find and identify the people they want to headhunt for roles. This means that the keywords you use across all of your social media platforms will have an impact on your chances of being found and recruited.

You might already be using Boolean search terms regularly online, so you may have an idea of how this works. Recruiters often use long, complex search strings, but these all follow basic Boolean search principles. To show you how companies might use Boolean searches in their ongoing quest to find suitable talent, take a look at these sample searches.

Using AND This will give a list of profiles in which all of the terms are present. For example:

- Finance AND Bloomberg AND London
- Textiles AND design AND graduate
- "Management systems" AND "organisational management"

Using OR This will broaden the search to include results that list either of the two or more words listed. This is often used when there are several ways of writing the same general skill set. For example:

- "Game designer" OR "games designer" OR "games programmer" OR programmer
- "Management consulting" OR "management consultant" OR consultant
- "Political research" OR "political researcher" OR "political analyst" OR "political analysis"

Using NOT This search will narrow the results by excluding particular terms. For example:

- International AND business NOT "international development"
- Engineer OR engineering NOT bioengineering
- "Graphic design" AND web NOT interior

You'll see that in some cases above, the terms are written within quotation marks. When searching for two or more words that form a phrase, use quotation marks around the words to make sure your results reflect what you're researching. If you're looking for social media blogs, a search for "social media blogs" will show you a list of blogs related to social media. If you ran that search without the quotation marks, your results would show blogs containing the word "social" and blogs containing the word "media". "Social media" would probably be somewhere in the mix, but the search results would also include irrelevant results. Use quotation marks to help make your searches more efficient.

Find more vacancies

The companies that run graduate recruitment programmes tend to be larger organisations. They typically hire for positions such as accountants, legal professionals, management consultants and other corporate roles. These companies have the budget to make sure they enter your radar through on-campus visits and advertising. The jobs they offer tend to be more on the "traditional" side, and it can sometimes seem that these are the only employment options available to graduates.

There are, however, many more opportunities for graduates than the large-scale graduate programmes that are heavily promoted on your campus. The world beyond graduate recruitment schemes is filled with less obvious career options, and roles in lesser known companies, which may be far more interesting to you. Small and medium enterprises, start-ups, charities, cultural organisations, publishing houses and a myriad of other organisations don't tend to hire along traditional graduate recruitment lines. This is because they don't have the same structure, budget or recruitment needs as large corporations. However, just because these businesses don't have 100 jobs for graduates every year does not mean they don't have opportunities.

Smaller businesses tend to have smaller budgets, and as a result, they advertise differently. Many will not think to alert local universities of their vacancies, but will use the main online job boards or choose specialised jobs boards for their sector. It costs money to advertise in those places. This is where social media comes in. It's free to post a tweet about a job in your company. It's free to write a LinkedIn or Facebook update saying, "We're hiring – check out this vacancy." The social job market exists somewhere in between the big shiny job boards and the hidden jobs market (more on that later).

There are several ways of finding out about these roles. One is to be connected to the right people; you can find out more about how to do this in Chapter 5. The other is to run searches on social media platforms to see which jobs are being advertised on social sites. You can use Twitter's search function at https://twitter.com/search-home to find jobs that have been shared on Twitter, or you can visit company pages on Facebook to see which organisations are hiring and the vacancies posted. LinkedIn has an entire section dedicated to job vacancies, including a student jobs portal at https://www.linkedin.com/studentjobs, which features graduate roles.

If you are already connected to some companies' social networks, whether that's by liking their Facebook pages or following them on Twitter, this can make it more likely that you will spot a vacancy when it comes up in your newsfeed, rather than having to remember to go to each individual company page on a regular basis. Graduate recruiters often share reminders on social media about graduate scheme closing dates, so connecting with their accounts is a good way to stay on top of all the application deadlines as well.

Exercise: Searching for jobs on Twitter

Go to https://twitter.com/search-home and enter keywords for the type of job you are looking for, for example, "job" AND "mechanical engineering" AND "plastics" AND "London". Find three relevant job possibilities. What are they?

Job opportunities found
1.
2.
3.

Understand career paths

Social media places a lot of information at your fingertips, helping you make informed decisions about the direction you want to take. Whether you are a current student or a recent graduate, the question "What are you going to do next?" has likely followed you at every turn. It can be very hard to find the answer to that question. Several pieces of information are required to figure out this puzzle. Chapter 2 on building your online brand addresses one piece of this puzzle, the piece that involves getting a good understanding of who you are, what you would like from your career and what you have to offer.

Another key piece of the puzzle is knowing what is out there. Equipping yourself with a good level of information about what jobs are available, and what's actually involved in the day-to-day of different roles, is a vital part of career decision making. This knowledge will put you in a much better position to decide which careers would suit you really well. You might think you know what certain jobs involve, but do you really?

There are so many misconceptions about the day-to-day realities of careers. Your view of a career could be affected by numerous factors. Your friends, classmates, family expectations and the portrayal of careers in the media can all influence your understanding of different career options. This can lead to an unrealistic view of certain jobs and could even make you discount a career that could be of real interest to you. It can be easy to quickly dismiss career options because of preconceived ideas you might have about them being too boring or difficult or unchallenging. You should always research jobs to understand what they really involve before you seriously pursue or discount them. LinkedIn profiles give a useful insight into what people actually work on in different roles, so they are a great place to start your career research.

What do people actually do?

As a student, you may have limited work experience; you might not have been exposed to a wide range of career options; and you might not even have heard of the sector in which you will find yourself working soon after university. Career options are changing so rapidly now that it's nigh on impossible to know what all the options are or what options there will be in a year or two from now.

There are so many kinds of jobs out there – with so many different types of organisations – that it can be overwhelming to try to figure out where to go next. You'll find a certain amount of information in the job descriptions in vacancy listings. However, if you only scratch the surface of the available information, you will never get a true picture of what the jobs actually entail, what they can offer you and which positions make the most sense for you.

You'll find more information in blogs, Twitter feeds and the LinkedIn accounts of people who are doing that kind work day-to-day. This is invaluable information when you are in the process of assessing prospective careers. If you have a few specific job types in mind, spend time identifying the people who do them, either by finding their names on company websites, by putting the job titles into a search engine or by looking them up through a keyword search on LinkedIn.

The more you research, the more you will develop a clear understanding of what different roles entail. You will then be able to use this knowledge to help you formulate decisions about your next steps. Keep a record of the things you find out. You could use a table like the one below to record your findings on each role that you research.

Exercise: Researching jobs

Using a search engine, find profiles of three people doing a job you have in mind, for example search for accountant CVs or "Accountant LinkedIn". Read through their profiles and note down what you find in the following table.

Job title
What qualifications do people in the job you want usually have?
Do people in this line of work usually have postgraduate qualifications or further training? If so, which courses?
Are there specialised skills that come up frequently in their profiles? List three that you have noticed:
1.
2.
3.

Chapter 4

Stand out in the hiring process

Great applications and interviews are about more than outlining everything that you can do. They also demonstrate your real interest in the company, your understanding of the sector and your enthusiasm for the role. With social media, the information available to you about what companies do and what they see as their unique offering is far broader than what you can find in the company's annual report or the "About us" section of their website.

In order to be a truly convincing candidate, you need to find out as much as you can about your target companies. The better an understanding you have of what makes them different, the better able you will be to convince an employer that you are serious about wanting to join their organisation. Well-researched evidence can be thoughtfully included in cover letters, application forms or at an interview.

When you're preparing an application or gearing up for an interview, find and read blogs about your sector, read Twitter feeds and LinkedIn bios of people who work in these companies, and gather as much information as you can to help you develop an interesting and robust answer to the inevitable question "Why do you want to work for our company?" This can make you stand out from other candidates. After all, companies want to hire people who want to work with *them*, not people who just want "any job".

There are many ways to creatively and effectively weave this information into your statements of interest or interview answers. Follow the exercise below to get started; then read the examples of how to incorporate your findings into great interview answers.

Exercise: Prove you really want to work for that employer

Pick a company you would like to work for. Read the following questions, and then check out their website and any social media channels they have. Record your observations in the boxes here.

What does this company believe they do better than others in the sector?

-

What do people who work there have to say about the company?
•
•

What interesting projects are staff working on?
•
•

Why are the facts you've listed above interesting to you?
•
•

During an interview, you are asked "Why do you want to work for this company?" If you did your research, you will know that this company puts great emphasis on nurturing careers. They prefer to hire someone for the long run and provide training to upskill their staff and help them progress up the ranks. With this in mind, your answer could look like this:

"I am motivated to find a career. I am not just looking for 'something to do' because my job is much more important than that. I'm looking for a role where I can constantly learn and develop my skill set, and I feel like your company would allow me to build a career that lasts into the future."

You are writing a statement of interest for a graduate traineeship in the marketing division of a large firm. From your research, you know that the company specialises in brand creation. So, you could include this knowledge in your statement in this manner:

> "I am interested in marketing as it encompasses so many interesting and creative ways of supporting business development, but I would particularly like to use my skills for brand creation as a I believe building a really strong brand image that consumers relate to is the keystone to building a business."

In an interview for a finance position, you are asked "What are your strengths?" You read in your research that the company places a strong emphasis on teamwork and interpersonal skills that are vital for working closely with others in a high-stress environment. You could show how you fit their brief by saying something like this:

> "I'm very driven to succeed, and I find I do my best work when I'm working in a team. I've always done well in individual projects in college, but my best grades have come from group work. I'm good at working with different types of people, understanding what they're good at and motivating team members to contribute to group tasks according to their strengths."

You would then need to give an example to back this statement up with solid evidence, but the point to retain here is that you can use social media to pick up on what companies want, and angle your responses accordingly.

As you can see, there are several ways you can incorporate what you have learned about a company into your applications and interviews. It can take a little bit of time to get a firm grasp of a company's culture, but the information is out there, clear to see on social media sites, so put yourself in a strong position by doing your research and then making the link clear to your prospective employers.

Get to know your interviewers

Interviews are nerve-wracking for even the most seasoned professional. However, the more prepared you are, the more in control you will feel when you're in the hot seat. Carrying out background research into the people who will be interviewing you can help you to accurately target your answers on the day. Read people's biographies on the company website by all means; but go beyond that, and look them up on other websites and social media channels as well. It's probably best, at this stage, to stick to LinkedIn and any professional blogs written by members of the panel. This is where people tend to share work-related material, and it's best to keep things on a professional footing at the interview. Find out what they do and what their achievements are, and gain an understanding of their main areas of focus in their work.

Equipped with this knowledge, you can build suitable content into your interview responses to display your real interest in the role. There is a fine line here. Put yourself in your interviewers' shoes, and think about what you would want to hear when they are asking questions. If you say you've read everything they've ever written, that might simply alarm them somewhat, because this could be moving into stalker territory. If you say that when you were researching the role, you came across a piece they wrote on a certain topic on a blog or in an online magazine, and share your thoughtful, positive reflections on that, this is much more likely to impress.

These strategies may seem very basic, but you would be surprised at how few people actually take advantage of all the information that is out there to be leveraged. This strategy provides you with a simple way to show that you are interested, and it can set you apart as a serious candidate, especially when competition is fierce.

Get hired for your social skills

The ability to successfully manage and promote yourself online is a skill that can be very attractive to employers. Social media branding and marketing are growing sectors, and because this is a relatively new development, many organisations are still learning how best to use it to promote their products and services. Increasingly, organisations are complaining that a lot of graduates tend to include "social media" as a skill in their CV and application, when it often emerges later that the applicant is not adept at online engagement at all. These graduates have social media accounts, but they're not managing them in a planned, strategic manner. In any application you send out, it's wise to stick to the "show, don't tell" mantra. Simply writing "social media" in your skills section won't create much of an impact.

Chapter 4

If you can show how well you brand and promote yourself online, employers will be interested in how you can do the same for their company. Follow the advice in this book to carefully cultivate your own online activities, and demonstrate that you have a good understanding of how to maximise the potential of key social media platforms.

From job search to on the job

Aim for balance while job searching

During your search for an internship or graduate role, you might identify a company that you'd really like to join. It's good to have a focus, but it's also important to keep your options open. Professing online how much you want to work for a certain company may well get you a job there – but if you're applying to (and being considered for) jobs in other companies, this approach could also lead to trouble.

No company wants to feel like a consolation prize. Do proactively follow your favourite companies on Twitter and like their company pages on LinkedIn and Facebook. Interact with their social media posts now and again within reason – don't like every single update as this creates an impression of desperation. Above all, aim for balance. If you overstate how much you want to work for a specific company, others may feel like you don't really want to work for them. Nobody wants to hire someone who is overzealous or appears too single-minded in his focus. On the other hand, companies are interested in hiring somebody who truly wants to join their team.

Be discrete

Discretion is paramount whenever you use social media. This is critical when job hunting. Recruitment practices are often kept highly confidential, and companies can react negatively to candidates who share too much about the process online. Candidates have been rejected because they divulged too much online during the hiring cycle.

A great online brand is as much about what you keep to yourself as it is about what you share. Discretion is an extremely important attribute of a good employee. If you share too much information online, could this indicate that you'll also divulge too much in a professional capacity? The finer details of companies' activities, projects and clients are often highly confidential and closely guarded. If you don't maintain a responsible, discreet approach to the information you possess, you could become a serious liability to your employer.

It's best not to post about interviews with specific companies online, and definitely keep your decision-making process to yourself. Tweeting "I have an offer from [company name A] but am waiting to hear back from [company name B] – what to do?" could be very detrimental to you. If either company reads this, any decision-making power you now have could quickly be taken out of your hands. It may be hard to believe but there are numerous reports of people doing this, and those stories did not end well for the indiscrete candidates. The best policy to adhere to, whenever you're wondering whether to post details of your interview, job offer or contract negotiations, is: if in doubt, don't post.

Social media when you have a job

People can see your social media posts, and when you're connected with a business, that company will want you representing them in the best possible manner. Employees can be great brand ambassadors for their company, so you can continue leveraging social media in a positive way once you have a job. You do need to be mindful of confidentiality, and many organisations have social media policies. It's important to read these so that you know what your employer expects. Once you identify yourself as the employee of a specific company, for example if you have indicated your company name on Facebook or listed it on LinkedIn or mentioned it in your Twitter bio, you could be deemed to be representing the company in everything that you share in a public forum online. Once you're clear on what you can and can't post, you could share updates about interesting projects and work trips that you go on, and keep sharing news and thoughts about developments in your industry. That kind of loyalty can reflect well on your company, but more importantly it can reflect very positively on you.

What to do next

If you have a good understanding of how social media can boost your job search, read on to Chapter 5 to learn how to make connections through social media to take this to the next level. If you're unsure

Chapter 4

about what type of job you would like to do, go through the exercises in Chapter 2 on "What have you got to offer?"

Useful websites

www.glassdoor.com is a website where employees rate their experience at various major companies, giving you inside information about their interview processes and what it's like to work there.

http://www.socialtalent.co/ is a social recruiting training agency that often shares useful advice for jobseekers on using social media to find work – look on the company blog and in the "Tools" section.

Career connections

Contents

There is a vast pool of students and graduates already out there looking for work, vying for attention. The work you will be doing to create social media profiles that show you in your best light will put you on a level playing field, which is important. However, if you want to make the most of social media in your job search, you can't set up your profiles and then log off, sit back and wait for things to happen. Take your online activity to the next level by being proactive and ensuring that your professional profile shows up on the radar of people who can help you in your job search. This chapter will take you through how to use social media to identify and connect with people who can open career doors for you.

Why networking matters

The hidden jobs market

Before getting into the nuts and bolts of how to network, you need to understand why it's helpful in your job search. You will probably search for opportunities on your career centre's vacancy page, individual companies' graduate recruitment pages and the mainstream job websites. In other words, you'll be doing what most people do when they look for work. It's definitely important to be looking in all of these places, but don't stop there. What you should be thinking about is how you can give yourself the best possible chance of being hired once you finish your course. This is where networking, and using social media to do that, can help.

There is a whole world of vacancies that never surface as job advertisements in any of the traditional channels. It's been estimated that up to 70 per cent of jobs are never advertised through traditional channels. This is what people refer to as the "hidden" jobs market. These unadvertised jobs aren't just floating in the ether: they are connected to people. So it naturally follows that the more people you are connected to, the more opportunities you are likely to hear about. The added advantage of hearing about job opportunities this way is that fewer people are looking in not-so-obvious places, so the competition will be less fierce. What's not to love?

Where employers look for employees

A company hires because it needs something. It has work that must be done, and needs a capable, trustworthy person to do it. Hiring through job advertisements means taking a shot in the dark, short-listing candidates based on a piece of paper. In an hour-long interview, interviewers ask candidates questions that they hope will give them a sense of whether this person they've never met will be a match for the job and the organisation. It is, to a certain extent, a guessing game – one where the stakes are high for both company and candidate. It is much easier, faster and cheaper for the company – and often far more reassuring – to hire someone who is known or has been recommended. The interview process still happens, but with an added layer of security: someone the interviewer already knows and trusts has vouched for the candidate. Hiring by referral can create an advantage for the company and for the jobseeker, who is already on the right person's radar and might get considered for a role she wouldn't have come across on a jobs website.

The following graph illustrates where companies look for candidates to fill vacant positions. Companies start at the bottom of the pyramid and work their way up. Most people searching for new jobs start at the top of the pyramid and work their way down. The more people who know you, know what you can do and what you want to do, the better your chance of hearing about vacancies that may never make it to the online job boards.

Chapter 5

How companies hire

Most jobseekers start their job search at the top of the pyramid, by looking at visible vacancies. Employers often start their search for candidates at the bottom of the pyramid, looking for referrals via their professional and personal networks. The more people you know working in your sector of interest, the more likely you are to hear about the so-called "invisible" vacancies that are circulated and filled without ever being advertised on the usual job boards.

Adverts

Recruitment Agencies

Professional Organisations

Word of Mouth

Contacts from Existing Staff

Internal Promotion

Chapter 5

Network to get ahead

The word "networking" can have negative connotations, as it is often seen as being synonymous with using people. There is definitely a certain type of networker who aggressively collects connections in a bid to work her way to the top, but this is not what you are being encouraged to do. Networking does not involve taking on the persona of a power-hungry, self-promoting person who is only out for herself. In fact, good networking is the exact opposite of this.

My social media story: Gayane Margaryan, Online Communications Associate, African Wildlife Foundation

When I was getting ready to graduate, I realised that I could get more meaningful interactions from employers by following and interacting with them on social platforms, instead of simply waiting for them to reply to my résumé or cover letter. With social media, I found a way to create a conversation and reach potential employers rather than just waiting for them to contact me.

I reached out to a manager with a high-profile advertising firm who was looking for an account executive. After our Twitter exchange, I was able to submit my résumé, using him as a reference, and secured two rounds of interviews. Using LinkedIn to search for job postings, I was able to connect with my future employer, a financial services non-profit in Washington, DC. LinkedIn allowed me to connect with my director-to-be, discover our mutual connections and showcase my experience and résumé. After sending him a LinkedIn message, I instantly received an interview request. If approached thoughtfully and considerately, using social media to network can give you a foot in the door.

The "hidden" jobs are more likely to come your way if people in your network know that you are looking for work and know what kind of job you are seeking. Social media makes it easy to quickly alert the people you know to your job search. Whichever social media platform you are using, there are ways to let your network know what you are looking for. You could write a post on Twitter or Facebook asking if any of your friends know anyone working in the green energy sector, for example. If you're hoping to move to another city or country, you could ask if anyone has any contacts in the location you have in mind.

Your existing network

Your network consists of the people you know, and networking simply means expanding that circle of people. Being a good networker means being aware of the people you know and lending a hand to them where you are able to do so. You probably do this all the time. Networking is not about keeping score, adding up help given versus help received. In all likelihood, you will have helped someone before who couldn't return the favour, and others may have helped you for nothing in return. For example, you might have sent somebody a link to an article that you thought would interest them, or told a friend about an unadvertised vacancy in a family friend's company to which this person could apply.

The people in your network may not know what you do or hope to do. You need to let people know you're searching for a job and to clearly communicate your career interests and aspirations. When people are aware of this information, you may come to mind when a suitable opportunity becomes available. If they don't know what you're looking for, they'll have no way of associating you with the opportunity and telling you that it exists.

Maintaining and communicating with your existing network is the easy part; it really just boils down to being thoughtful towards your circle of friends and any colleagues you have. Expanding your network can be more challenging because it involves going out of your comfort zone and connecting with people you have never met. This can feel intimidating.

Your extended network

It's clichéd to say that it's a small world, but it's very true. Social media simply makes the world smaller again. Connections can become a vital key to opening doors, and you will find that it can be much quicker to have someone open a door for you than to try to break it down with a barrage of CVs. The chances are that there is somebody in your extended network who can help you out by giving you advice or introducing you to someone who can. You probably have very little concept of who your friends' friends are or who your former colleagues' contacts are. In all likelihood, you know people who are studying all kinds of different things – people you went to school with who are now attending different universities and studying many different subjects. Do you know everyone they know? Probably not. You would be amazed at the contacts that are just one degree of separation away.

People who know people you know are what LinkedIn calls your "second-degree connections". You probably know dozens, if not hundreds of people, and each of those people has their own immediate network of connections. The people in that outer circle can be incredibly useful in your job search. You might not directly know

Chapter 5

anybody doing the type of work you would like to do or working in one of your target companies, but there is a strong possibility that friends of friends might tick those boxes.

Once you identify and connect with those individuals, they can advise you about your sector of interest and tell you about what their jobs involve. If they're working in a company you want to work for, they might be able to provide a few tips as to what that organisation really looks for in candidates. This information can be invaluable in helping you to target your application and your interview responses. There is a gold mine of information out there which can assist you to get to the job you want. Quite often, it's simply a matter of finding someone who can help and asking in the right way.

Finding people who can help

Social media makes finding people who can help you out so much easier than ever before. LinkedIn, Facebook and Twitter are particularly useful in this context. It's easier to connect with someone who is connected to someone you know than to contact with somebody "cold", so being able to see who is in your extended network on social media platforms is very useful.

If you were looking to find somebody working as a researcher in a think tank for example, you could log into LinkedIn and search for "research" AND "think tank". The list of results that come up will show you people in your network first, so it will show you people with those keywords in their profiles with whom you have some connection. You can narrow down the results by location, company and other filters on the left-hand side of the screen. You can also click on someone's profile to see how you are connected to that person. If you would like to get in touch with him, you can send an email to your mutual contact or use LinkedIn's introduction request feature, asking him to connect you with the person you'd like to contact. LinkedIn shows you both second connections – people connected to your immediate network – and third connections – people who are connected to people who are connected to your network. As you can see, the third connections are a more tenuous link, so you may have more success trying to get in touch with second connections.

LinkedIn limits the number of people searches you can do each month with a free account. However you can get around this by going to the "Find Alumni" function, located under the "Connections" tab, where you can carry out unlimited searches to find alumni from specific universities. You can use this to find out where graduates from your course have been after they finished their studies. This is incredibly useful information. The reason the Alumni tool is particularly relevant in a networking context is that there are likely thousands of alumni from your university, all at different career stages, already on LinkedIn. Even if you don't have a contact in common, you do have the fact that you are from the same university, and this can be enough of an opener that could make somebody more likely to respond to your connection request.

Aside from the fact that this tool helps you to identify people you could approach, it is one of the most exciting developments in social media for anyone considering career options. You can get access to the profiles of hundreds of people doing the kind of work you would love to do and read through their profiles to find out how they got there and what qualifications they have. It's an incredibly useful source of careers information that you should spend time exploring. You can filter the results according to what course someone has studied, although LinkedIn uses standardised course categories, so you might get more relevant results by running a search for your course in the Alumni page's search bar, with your course title in quotation marks. You can also filter alumni by where they live (useful if you're trying to expand your network internationally and targeting a career overseas), what company they work for, what they do, what they're skilled at and how you're connected. In short, this is an incredibly powerful and easy way to find alumni you could connect with who share your connection to your university.

Facebook also makes it easy to find people working at specific companies. When you are doing your research into a company, log onto Facebook and see if you can find anybody working there who could give you the inside track. Simply go to the search bar and search for "people who work at [company name]". Indicating your location can help to make the results more relevant to you. You can then filter the results to "people", and you will see a list of people on Facebook who work at that company. People with whom you have a connection in common will be listed first. So if this search locates a few people in your extended network who are already at your target company, you can see who your mutual contact is and ask whether this person could make the introduction.

Similarly, you can run a keyword search in Twitter's search box, where you list the company's name and location – particularly useful if you're applying to a multinational and want to identify people in the office closest to where you want to work. Then filter your search results by clicking "Accounts" to see a list of people on Twitter who have that company name and that location in their Twitter bio. You could then start following them and interacting with them on the platform by liking or responding to their updates. Twitter has also made it possible for users to choose to allow anyone on Twitter to send them a Direct Message, which is a private message to another Twitter user. If the person you are interested in speaking to has this function enabled, you could message her directly. However, this might come slightly out of the blue so interacting with her updates first is probably a better approach.

How to network effectively

Effective networking is not rocket science. You network all the time whenever you meet people and talk to them. That's what it boils down to in essence. The term "networking" seems to have imbued this basic social interaction with a strange aura that causes people to feel that it's a dark and manipulative art. It's not. It simply involves interacting with others. Students are sometimes afraid because they feel they have "nothing to say". Worry less about what you have to say and more about building a good relationship with the person you are speaking to for advice or guidance. You build good relationships by asking people about their experience and the work that they do – all people like to talk about themselves. So instead of worrying about what you have to say, think about what intelligent questions you can ask somebody you are introduced. You'll learn more about that later on in this chapter.

Like many students, you might feel intimidated by the prospect of getting in touch with someone you don't know. You might be concerned about inconveniencing someone. You may also fear that, because you're relatively inexperienced, you will be asking for help that you won't be able to reciprocate. The reality is that there will often be times when you won't be able to return the favour to someone who has helped you; but networking is more of a "pay it forward" concept. Somebody might help you now, and in a year or two, when you've established yourself in your career, you'll be eager to help the next generation of students looking for advice.

People are generally inclined to help others. If you feel that the thought of contacting someone you've never met to ask for advice is going too far, think again. It's all about how you frame it. The first rule of networking is that you are not asking anybody for a job. Asking for a job is a lot to ask, and most people are not in a position to influence corporate hiring and budgets to any great extent. The reason you're contacting people is to find out more about the jobs out there. You're trying to obtain the insight of someone who works in the sector who can share his experience with you. He was once in your shoes, trying to get a foot in the door; so hearing about how he broke into a particular industry can give you some extremely helpful ideas.

Making the connection

If you have identified somebody you would like to speak to, or somebody has said, "I know someone who can help you, and I'll introduce you", you need to think about what you want to say when you make the initial contact with that person. Whether you send an email or make a phone call, you don't want to spend the whole time talking about yourself, particularly when you're only speaking to her for the first time. Put yourself in the other person's shoes. This individual doesn't know you and she probably isn't that interested in knowing all about you — not out of mean-spiritedness, but because people are busy and have many things going on at once. Therefore, you need to make the interaction as pleasant and easy for the other person as possible.

Think about the kind of message that you would respond to if you received it out of the blue. You probably wouldn't react too favourably to somebody getting in touch with you and saying:

> Hello, I'm a final year student looking for a job in your company. Can you give me some advice?
>
> Martin

That message is very focused on the person writing it, and is asking a lot. Compare that to the following approach:

> Hi Claire,
>
> I'm a final year student at [university name] and see you graduated from the same course as me a few years ago. Looking at your profile, you seem to be doing really interesting work with [company]. I'm really keen to work for them and would love to connect with you and hear about your experience working there. If you would be willing to share your insight, it would be great if I could give you a quick call at a time that works for you. I appreciate you're likely very busy, so completely understand if this doesn't suit. Let me know what you think, and thank you for your time.
>
> Kind regards,
>
> Martin

The second message is much more likely to get a response. It is not assuming that help will be given; it's not pushy; and it's also flattering to the person being addressed. Another important point is that Martin is respectful of Claire's time and is not asking for too much. Use this as a guide when you try to contact people. Be considerate, don't ask for too much, and be complimentary. If you've never done this before, it can seem a little bit difficult, but once you do it a few times and get positive responses, it will become so much easier, and you will learn so much from the people who do respond and who help you by sharing their advice and guidance.

Not everybody you contact is going to say yes. People are busy, and some people simply aren't interested. That's fine, and don't be disheartened if you get no response from a few people. However, if you find that you've contacted a lot of people and nobody has responded, you might want to review how you're approaching people. Try asking a friend or a career adviser to take a look at the emails you are sending and get their feedback to make sure you're on the right track.

Informational interviewing

Social media has dramatically augmented our ability to locate and communicate with people in any walk of life. From a career-exploration point of view, this is probably its most significant benefit. If there is something you dream of becoming after you graduate, but you don't know anyone in your circle who's doing that kind of work – or who could possibly advise you – social networks can open up a world of professionals who can help. It's likely that there is somebody out there doing something similar to what you are considering. Through reading this person's LinkedIn profiles, tweets or blogs, you can begin to understand how you might set out on a similar career path. You could take this a step further by contacting the person to see whether he might be willing to share advice with you. You could be pleasantly surprised at how many people are happy to give up their time and share their knowledge with complete strangers.

Carrying out informational interviews is a brilliant way to gather real information about different careers while also expanding your network. You can't ask people you don't know to give you a job (well, you can, but it's unlikely to work most of the time), but you can ask them for advice. Informational interviewing is exactly that: interviewing people to gain information about careers in a given field.

Once you've made contact with the people you'd like to speak to, plan what you'd like to ask them, so you can make the best possible use of your opportunity – and their time. Here are a few examples of questions you could ask:

1. What do you enjoy about your job?
2. What's the most challenging part of your work?
3. How did you decide that this was the job you wanted to do?
4. Did you complete any specific training that you feel helped you to get this job?
5. What strategy would you suggest I use to get my foot in the door in this sector?
6. Is there anyone else you think I should talk to in order to find out more about this kind of work?

It is always a good idea to ask whether they know anybody else you could talk to for advice. Professionals tend to have strong networks

Chapter 5

within their own sector, and they could connect you to other people who can give you further insight and advice.

Before you make contact with somebody, think about what you hope to get out of the conversation to make the most of the contact. Jot down your ideas in the table below.

Exercise: Preparing for an informational interview

What do you hope to gain from the conversation? Is there specific knowledge you want to gain about necessary qualifications and key trends in a specific sector, or do you want to find out about the culture in that person's company so you can tailor your application or interview technique? Write down the top three things you hope to learn through the conversation, and keep these to hand so you don't forget.

Three things I hope to learn from the informational interview:

1.
2.
3.

Don't be a stalker

This is good advice for life in general, but it applies to social media and job hunting as well. The Internet makes it very easy to investigate people's backgrounds. A certain amount of online snooping can enhance your job search, but there are limits. If you're constantly looking at the same person's profile on LinkedIn and haven't adjusted your privacy settings, she will get an alert every time, and this could make her quite uncomfortable. Similarly, if you're trying to connect with somebody you don't know, don't bombard her with messages or compulsively retweet all of her tweets. All of these things can scare people away.

Exercise caution in terms of how you use any information you find online. If you've done extensive research about the people interviewing you, use this information to tailor your answers to their interests. You've gone too far if you start referring to the photos of their children that you managed to unearth on Facebook, or if you decide to compliment a senior manager on an award he won back in university. This may seem like common sense, but these are things that many educated, qualified, potentially great applicants have done. If you're not sure where the line is, think about how you might react if the tables were turned. For example, if your interviewer said that she saw the photographs you posted online of your last holiday and asked you how you enjoyed it, you might feel a little uncomfortable. If you're wondering whether something is a little bit "too much", it probably is.

Saying thank you

When you have connected with someone who has provided you with help or advice, it's critical to remember to say thank you. The best way to do this is to send a handwritten card or note thanking the person for their time and help. This might sound terribly old-fashioned, but it takes time, thought and effort, and it's a gesture that shows you truly value the information and help you have received. You can send a text or email thanking the person immediately after speaking to him, but don't stop there. The person you've spoken to has given you his time, with no expectation of anything in return. A little bit of gratitude can go a long way, and you never know when that person may be able to help you again, for example in the future when a role comes up that you would be well suited to perform.

Think of others following in your footsteps and wishing to talk to that person for the same reasons you did. Not taking the time to acknowledge the help you've received could sour her experience of helping new graduates, and she might not be so willing to help next time. For your own sake, for the sake of the professional you've spoken to and for the sake of others – just say thanks.

What to do next

If you're ready to start networking online, head to Chapters 6 through 9 to find out how to do that on different social media platforms. If you want to learn more about how businesses use social media to hire, take a look at Chapter 4 on boosting your job search.

Useful websites

www.hbr.com *Harvard Business Review's* website is updated daily and features the latest news about everything from marketing to career planning, and a lot more besides. This website is one to check into regularly for inspiration and ideas.

www.forbes.com Forbes is a great resource for jobseekers and often shares articles from HR managers and other thought leaders in the recruitment arena which frequently include networking advice.

keithferrazzi.com This is the website Keith Ferrazzi, author of *Never Eat Alone*, the go-to book on networking. The website includes free resources.

Make the most of LinkedIn

Contents

If you choose only one social network to enhance your job search, make it LinkedIn. With over 350 million members, it is the largest and most respected professional network online, and it can be a very powerful instrument for you.

Overview

LinkedIn is important for a number of different reasons:

Millions of career paths If you have a dream job in mind but aren't sure how to get it, LinkedIn is a great place to do some research. Search for the profiles of people who are doing the job you would love to do, to see how they have built up their experience through professional roles and further study.

Millions of contacts Opportunities are connected to people. The more connections you have, the more likely it is you'll hear about interesting opportunities from those connections.

Over 3 million companies Businesses can set up their own pages on LinkedIn where they share company news and information about vacancies. You can also see a list of all the company's employees who are on LinkedIn and click to view their profiles. In addition, LinkedIn lets you see what vacancies are available in companies you're connected with through your network. You could use this information to get in touch with someone in your target company and to give yourself an edge when applying for a new role.

Employers searching for candidates Research has found that 89% of companies have hired someone through LinkedIn.[9] Give yourself the chance to be found if an employer is searching for someone with your skills.

Your online CV LinkedIn provides a user-friendly, professional-looking platform where you can set out your stall to impress any employers taking a look.

As you can see, LinkedIn ticks a lot of boxes for the jobseeker. It provides a careers database, a way to manage and expand your network, a platform to develop a professional profile online and a way to find and apply to vacancies.

Paid or unpaid membership?

One of the first questions students ask is whether they need to upgrade to a paid membership. There's really no need to pay for an account if you're looking for work. LinkedIn's main source of income stems from companies who pay large sums of money to access the profiles of potential employees.[10] They spend this money because they are working to headhunt professionals who usually have some experience and a well-established skill set. Invest time in creating a keyword-rich, All-Star profile that clearly shows what you have to offer, and you will have an impressive professional online presence for free.

The extras that come with a paid membership, such as being able to view more profiles when you perform a people search, or being able to see a list of everyone who has viewed your profile in the past three months, probably aren't worth the investment because they won't really help you in your job search. So, for now, work with the free version and invest time in building a well-written profile. See the example on pages 83–85.

Get set up

LinkedIn profiles are composed of a number of key sections, each with a specific title and purpose. Take a look at the sample profile on the following pages to understand the key elements of a profile.

Maria Smith
Final year Politics, Philosophy and Current Affairs
student interested in policy analysis and research careers
United Kingdom | International Affairs

Previous   Atlantic Community
Education   UCL

Send Maria InMail ▼

0
connections

☆   https://uk.linkedin.com/pub/maria-smith/b9/a23/238

Background

 Summary

I'm a final year student with a strong interest in international relations and political affairs. I have gained an indepth understanding of the core concepts in international affairs, and developed skills in qualitative and quantitative analysis through my course assignments. I will be graduating in September 2015 with a predicted Honours Degree and aim to begin my career working in a think tank or policy research role in the greater London area.

 Experience

Online Moderator
Atlantic Community
June 2014 – September 2014 (4 months)

Atlantic Community is an online foreign policy think tank with over 8000 members.
I reviewed up to 800 comments a week and assessed their suitability prior to publishing on the site.
I was the first point of contact for any technical issues that arose in the comments section and resolved these by liaising with the IT department.
I identified ways the think tank could better promote itself to university students, and developed and managed a social media marketing campaign targetting UCL as a pilot. High levels of student engagement with the campaign led to its roll-out to other universities across Europe after my departure.

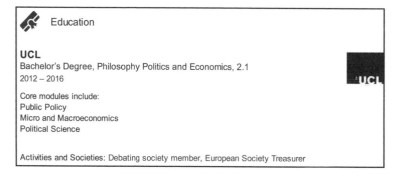 Education

UCL
Bachelor's Degree, Philosophy Politics and Economics, 2.1
2012 – 2016

Core modules include:
Public Policy
Micro and Macroeconomics
Political Science

Activities and Societies: Debating society member, European Society Treasurer

Chapter 6

The High School
A Levels, History, English, Politics, French, Received As in all subjects
2008 – 2013

Trained twice weekly in the evenings and played matches every Saturday during the school year.

Activities and Societies: Player on the Girls' Senior Hockey Team

---

Additional Info

- **Interests**

Interational Relations, International Politics, EU Affairs

Skills

Policy Analysis

Qualitative Research

International Relations

Political Science

Public Policy

Global Citizenship

Ethics

Languages

English   **French**

Volunteer Experience & Causes

Treasurer
The European Society, UCL
September 2014 – Present (1 year 1 month)

Manage society's annual budget. Allocate funds for society events by assessing suitability of proposed events and their alignment with the society's core strategy. I have demonstrated the ability to navigate differing agendas in order to ensure that the society promotes itself in a way which is consistent with its aims at all times.

Opportunities Maria is looking for:

• Skills-based volunteering (pro bono consulting)

Causes Maria cares about:

• Politics

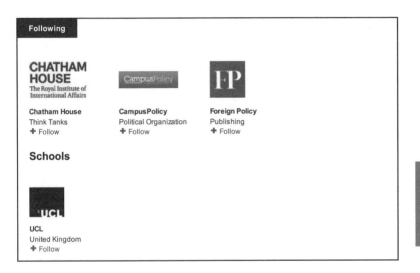

Setting up an account

Setting up your LinkedIn account isn't difficult. Follow these quick steps:

1. Go to https://www.linkedin.com. Fill out your first name, last name and email address. Then, create a password and click "Join Now".

2. Select the option that fits your current situation, and you will be prompted to input the following details:

   Employment: Enter information about your current employment.

   Jobseeker: Input details of your most recent employment. If you do not have previous work experience, you can include a volunteer role here for now if you would like to do so.

   Student: Provide your education details.

3. Link your address book.

At this point, LinkedIn will ask you for access to your email address book. This can be useful, as it will make it easier for you to find people you already know on the social media site. Once you link your email contacts to your LinkedIn profile, you will receive a prompt asking you if you want to send invitations to connect with all of those people. Although this might seem like a great way to acquire many connections quickly, resist. Clicking "yes" will send a generic "I'd like to add you to my network" message to every single one of your contacts, and that isn't a great idea.

In fact, this is a pretty bad idea for two reasons. First, LinkedIn is about building and maintaining relationships, and an impersonal connection request will do you no favours in the eyes of the people who receive them. Secondly, there are all kinds of people in your address book, from your exes to your lecturers, to the person you emailed four years ago to see if he had a room to rent. It's unlikely that you want to connect with all these people. Hold off until you have time to send out personalised invitations to connect.

These are the absolute basics of getting started. Now you need to familiarise yourself with the different privacy options, and then you can start building your profile step by step.

Privacy settings

One of the greatest things about LinkedIn is the wealth of information it provides. Reading the profiles of other professionals can give you myriad ideas as to how to conduct your job search now and in the future. It can also provide inspiration when you're trying to establish what to write on your own profile.

Before you start investigating what other people have written on their profiles, it's worth changing LinkedIn's default privacy settings. When you look at someone else's profile, they receive an alert saying that you have viewed it. Although this can work to your advantage if someone receives that notification in certain situations at this stage, you're just looking for ideas, so it's probably best to do so anonymously.

To change your privacy settings, hover your mouse over the small profile photo box on the upper right-hand side of the page. A list will pop up. Click "Privacy and Settings – Review". Then, go to the

"Profile" box, and click "Select what others see when you have viewed their profile." You will have three options from which to choose.

Option 1: Your name and headline When this option is selected, any time you look at another person's profile, she will receive an alert that says "[Your Name] has viewed your profile." Every time you look at someone's profile, the person will receive a notification, so if you're thinking of repeatedly checking somebody's profile, it's not a good idea to use this setting. If someone receives notifications that you're looking at his profile every day – or several times a day – he might feel a little uncomfortable.

If you particularly want to come to somebody's attention on LinkedIn, this setting can be useful. The other advantage of using this setting is that you'll also receive notifications telling you who's looked at your profile. This can be valuable. You can turn on the anonymous setting – option 3 – when you log into LinkedIn, and then switch back to option 1 when you log out. That way you'll still get to find out who has visited your LinkedIn page, without letting others know you've been looking at theirs.

Option 2: Anonymous profile characteristics, such as industry and title If you look at the profile of someone while using this setting, the person will receive an alert notifying them that someone in a certain industry sector has viewed their profile. For example, if your profile states that you are in the education industry, the alert will read: "Someone in the education industry viewed your profile". This setting does not provide complete anonymity; a person can click to see a list of people who are listed on LinkedIn within that industry. Your name will be among them, but it could be one of thousands, so there is an element of privacy.

Option 3: Being completely anonymous This is probably the most advisable setting when you are setting up your profile. Though your profile is incomplete, you will want to keep your views of other people's profiles anonymous. If someone gets a notification that you have looked at her profile, curiosity might lead her to click on your name and read yours. If she clicks through to find an incomplete profile, this won't tell her anything about you, so it's a lost opportunity. The downside of this setting is that you won't receive notifications of who is viewing your profile either.

Chapter 6

All-Star profiles: Why and how

What's an All-Star profile, and why do I need one?

LinkedIn rates your profile, from Beginner to All-Star, based on the completeness of the information you provide. All-Star profiles are given priority in search results. For example, if a recruiter wants to hire a graduate who has studied international business and speaks French, she could run a search for candidates containing those keywords in their profiles. The first pages of results will be filled with people who have those words in their profiles and have All-Star profiles.

If you don't have an All-Star profile, your profile will be so far down the search results that it is unlikely ever to be seen. When was the last time you looked at the fourth page of Google search results? Probably a long time ago, if ever. The same holds true for people looking for candidates like you on LinkedIn. Although you are unlikely to be headhunted at this stage, it's still helpful to try to meet LinkedIn's All-Star criteria. A good LinkedIn profile is one that includes all the elements required to reach that status.

To create an All-Star profile, you will need to populate the key sections of your profile and provide specific information, including the following:

- A profile picture
- A headline
- A summary
- Over 50 connections
- Your target industry and location
- Your current position, with details of your activities and achievements
- Two previous positions (these can include volunteer work)
- Your education
- Your key skills (at least three).

The rest of this chapter will take you through all of the above, and more.

Hit the right note with your profile picture

Your profile picture is one of the main things people look at when they view your profile. Your profile is 14 times more likely to be viewed if you include a picture[11]. However, not all pictures are suitable, and it's important to convey the right impression from the start.

You don't need to spend money on a professional headshot, but you equally don't want to use a grainy, cheesy photo or a selfie. Aim for something in between. A photo of you appearing approachable and professional is all you really need.

Profile photos: Common mistakes to avoid

To ensure you choose the best profile picture possible, here are some common mistakes to avoid.

Group photos   Nobody will know who you are.

Photos from a night out   Although you may look lovely in the clothes you wore to your cousin's wedding, you won't seem professional in a strapless dress and heavy make-up, or in a tuxedo.

Photos with other people cropped out   A photograph featuring you leaning on a headless shoulder looks unprofessional and makes it appear that you are too lazy to take a photograph that is more suitable – this is not the message you want to send.

Funny photographs   These can sometimes work if you're an established professional or if you're looking for work in more creative sectors. However, if you're a student or recent graduate trying to get your foot in the door of more straight-laced companies, you run the risk of putting off more employers than you attract.

Over-the-top attempts at looking professional   A photograph of you standing at a podium delivering a speech or staring intently at an annual report doesn't so much say "I'm a professional and you really need me in your company" as "I'm trying too hard to look important".

Selfies   Pictures that you clearly took of yourself with your mobile phone have become something of a joke, and they certainly will not portray you as "professional". LinkedIn is trying to encourage more people to upload photographs by promoting the idea of a "work selfie"; however, if you look at the examples of photographs in that campaign, you can't even tell they are selfies. So stick to photographs taken by someone else to ensure you create as professional an impression as possible.

Choose your profile picture carefully. It is the first thing viewers will see, so it needs to set the right tone. The image you are aiming for is of a friendly, professional person, without being try-hard.

Eye-catching headlines

Your headline is one of the key elements of your profile. When somebody performs a search on LinkedIn, this is the information that appears:

Maria Smith `YOU`
Final year Politics, Philosophy and Current Affairs student interested in policy analysis and research careers
United Kingdom • International Affairs

Your headline is the text that appears directly below your name. An employer looking at the results of a keyword search will make decisions about whether to click on a profile based on very limited information. Create an interesting headline that will make people want to find out more about you. If you have a boring or incomplete headline, you could be overlooked.

When you include details of your current job or course of study in the main body of your profile, LinkedIn automatically puts this information into your headline. The problem is that this often doesn't provide useful information about what you can do or the type of role you're hoping to find.

If you're seeking a graduate management consultant role after your course, a headline that reads "Student at University of Exeter" or "Sales Assistant at Smith's Newsagents" is not going to give employers any reason to click on your profile. You have the option to edit your headline, and doing so can improve the look of your profile. There is only space for 120 characters in this section, so it can take a bit of time to formulate a strong message in just a few short words.

The evolution of a headline Here is an example of a headline evolving from poor to keyword-rich:

The evolution of a headline	
Poor headline	Student at University of Exeter
Average headline	BA Business and French student interested in management consultancy opportunities
Good headline	Chair of BizSoc, First-Class Honours BA. Business and French student seeking graduate management consultancy role

With only 120 characters to work with, how do you create a compelling headline? Follow the six steps listed here to make this happen.

Exercise: Six simple steps to headline success

To create your headline, follow these steps. It might seem like a lot of work for a mere 120 characters, but you need to get them right.

1. Go to "Edit profile" and hover your mouse over the headline section. You will see an option to "See what others with your background are saying in their headlines". Click on this.

2. Read the first ten headline suggestions, and write down the top two that stand out to you:

   1.

   2.

3. Now, think about the kind of job you would like. Put the job title in LinkedIn's search bar, and filter your search results by "people". Look at the headlines in the first two pages of search results. Write down the three headlines you find the most interesting:

   1.

   2.

   3.

4. Look at the headlines you have selected. What do they have in common? What makes them great? What elements do you want to incorporate into your profile?

   1.

   2.

   3.

5. Look back at the keyword exercise you completed in Chapter 2. List the two keywords you would like to incorporate into your headline statement.

1.

2.

6. Now that you've done all your research, try to come up with your own unique headline:

My headline:

Secrets of a great summary

The summary section provides a great opportunity for you to introduce yourself to anyone reading your profile. Many people skip this section of their profile, but it is incredibly important. If you're looking for a job, customise your summary by highlighting your relevant skills and experience. State the kind of job you're looking for, along with your availability. Writing a good summary can be the most time-consuming part of developing your profile, but it's worth doing well.

Write this, and all of your profile, in the first person. You might come across LinkedIn summaries written in the third person, in the same style as an author biography in a book. This isn't a great idea, as everyone knows you write your own summary, so it can come across as slightly pretentious when written in the third person. The other reason to use the first person is that you're trying to connect with people, and it's easier to do this when you talk directly to the person who's reading what you have to say.

The guidelines for this section are similar to those used for a cover letter. Your summary should comprise two to three short paragraphs describing your unique set of skills and your career interests. If it's longer than this, people will likely skip past it. You may believe that as a student or recent graduate, you don't have much to say here. At this early stage in your career, you're not expected to have an extensive work history. What you do have is your education as well as your experience and transferable skills. Remember, these are skills you have developed as a result of your coursework, part-time work, involvement in societies, volunteer work and other extracurricular activities such as sports. All the work you did in Chapter 2 to define your online brand will come into play now.

The following example of a summary evolving from poor to powerful will help you understand what to aim for in your own summary.

Evolution of a summary	
Poor summary	Hardworking and enthusiastic graduate looking for an opportunity that will challenge me and where I can develop my skills.
Average summary	As a soon-to-be graduate with a degree in history and French, I'm interested in graduate opportunities in a business where I can use my language skills. I'm particularly interested in working with small and medium enterprises expanding into the French market.
Good summary	I am a fluent English and French speaker with experience working in a marketing role with several small businesses. From setting up and managing a successful social media marketing campaign for a London-based craftsperson who was entering the French market to carrying out market research for my university while working part-time during my studies, I have a good understanding of the importance of knowing what the market wants and the skills to develop a marketing campaign accordingly.
	I really enjoy working in small teams, and in my work experience to date I have demonstrated that I thrive in busy environments where I can come up with creative ideas to help further business goals. I will be graduating with a degree in history and French in September, and I am currently searching for my next role. I am keen to bring my language skills, social

> media knowledge and marketing know-how to a
> company that is expanding into international markets.
> If you would like to contact me about opportunities in
> your business, you can connect with me here or send
> me an email at janedoe@emailaddress.com.

Can you see the difference? The first summary is generic, using clichéd words like "hardworking" and "enthusiastic" without providing any evidence to underline these claims. It's also completely unclear what type of role the person wants. The average summary gives more detail but is very brief. This is a missed opportunity for the student to really make an impression.

In the good summary, the student writes in more detail about what she is capable of doing as well as what she will bring to a business. At the same time, she keeps things brief, clear and concise so that the summary will actually be read and not ignored because of its length.

So, work carefully on your summary to ensure you do the following:

- Show your capabilities.
- Explain your interests.
- Outline skills that could help a business.
- List your contact details.
- Prove that you would be a valuable asset.

Remember that you are selling yourself to potential employers, so give them a reason to "buy" what you have to offer.

To help you make the most of your summary, here is a simple summary builder that you can use. Answer each question, and when you're done, you'll have all of the components of your summary. You just need to put it all together.

Employers are people, and they want to hire people. Don't be afraid to inject enthusiasm into your summary. The tone to aim for here is somewhat formal, but also friendly and engaging. Let the people reading your profile gain a sense of who you are and what kind of colleague you would be.

It's a great idea to include a "call to action" at the end of your summary, directly inviting people to connect with you. Consider including your

Exercise: Summary builder

Start putting together key points for your summary by answering the following questions.

What kind of job are you seeking?

What are the skills and experience employers want from people who perform this job? If you're still not sure, do some more research on jobs boards, including your university's graduate vacancy page.

Look at the above list. What skills and experience do you have that match?

What achievements can you write about that prove you have what it takes to do this job? Think about what you have achieved in university courses, part-time work, involvement with student societies, volunteer work, sports teams, etc.

email address here. LinkedIn is set up so that you can only connect with people whose email addresses you already have. If a potential employer outside of your network wants to talk to you, he will have to pay a small fee to LinkedIn in order to send you a connection request. Provide your email address so potential employers can avoid this hurdle. This will make it much easier for them to get in touch with you.

Explaining your education

As a student or recent graduate, one of your key selling points is the level and quality of the education you have gained. LinkedIn makes it easy for you to showcase your education, past and present. The first thing to do is to fill in the name of your course, the name of the institution and the dates you attended college. You could stop there – but that would not be making the most of this opportunity.

The education section is a great place to include more of your keywords and demonstrate your focus. Consider listing the ranking of your university or of the department you studied within. This can be particularly useful if you are looking for work internationally, as people will not necessarily be familiar with your institution, even if it is highly ranked and well known locally.

When it comes to writing about the courses you've taken and noting your grades, there are two options. You can record your overall course grade, along with the subjects you studied, in the text box under your education. Alternatively, you can list your courses separately in the "Courses" section. Whichever option you choose, think about the subjects you want to highlight. Resist the temptation to list every single subject you studied, as nobody will take the time to wade through a long list. Think about the image you are trying to create, and pick out the subjects that best reflect this. For example, if you have a business degree and are targeting a graduate role in recruitment, you could list your degree title followed by relevant subjects such as "Introduction to organisational psychology", "Human resource management" and "Intercultural organisation management".

Students and graduates often fall into the trap of including a long description of courses in this section. You might come across text on some profiles along these lines: "This course focuses upon developing students' capacity to think critically and enhances participants' skills in a range of areas including research, presentation skills and written communication skills."

This type of information is not particularly useful to employers and reads more like an advertisement for the course than for you.

Remember that LinkedIn is about showcasing all that *you* have to offer. A more useful approach is to write a few lines about the skills you have developed during the course. Write in the first person and, as in a CV, provide evidence for each statement. The boxed example shown here shows you how to do this.

> Developed excellent public speaking skills through preparation and delivery of presentations to small class groups on a regular basis throughout the course, in addition to presenting thesis project to over 60 fellow students and academics in final year.
>
> Demonstrated the ability to critically analyse a large amount of information and present complex arguments clearly and concisely in term papers, and consistently achieved Honours for written work submitted.
>
> Elected class representative in final year, and advocated on behalf of class as issues arose. Managed a successful negotiation process with senior department staff which led to the scheduling of "refresher" lectures before final examinations.

Employer's view: Orla Heffernan, HR Business Partner, Coca-Cola Hellenic Ireland and Northern Ireland

LinkedIn is a medium we use to connect with prospective employees and to raise awareness of our annual Graduate Programme. It connects students and recent graduates to information on our organisation and provides a platform for two-way communication. Students and graduates should develop a professional network and maintain a professional profile. Always include a LinkedIn summary, as this calls out to the reader to take notice. If there is an educational qualification advantage, locate "Education" after the "Summary" section and before "Work Experience". Always put a LinkedIn URL at the top of a CV. A recruiter will cross-check a CV with a LinkedIn profile. Make sure the details match, and include a professional rather than social photo.

Experience

The experience section is where you can list any substantial experience you have had to date. This doesn't need to be paid work. In fact, it's best to step away from categorising your experience into paid and unpaid. Think instead of anything you have done where you have had an impact and demonstrated skills. You can include volunteer work within this section, or list it separately in the volunteering section.

Similarly to a CV, you want the most relevant experience to be visible as early as possible, so if you have unpaid experience doing something closely linked to the roles you're applying for, consider listing it in the "Experience" section. This will position it higher up on the page, so anyone scrolling through your profile will quickly see this.

You can write about your experience in the same format as you would on a CV, using brief bullet points, or you can write a brief paragraph or two outlining your experience. There is no hard rule about the best approach here, and it comes down to personal preference. Whichever format you choose, you need to keep a few key principles in mind.

Provide context Not everybody will have heard of the places you have worked, so it's always a good idea to start any description of experience with a line or two stating what the business does. For example, were you working in a small law firm specialising in probate, or were you working for a large law firm with corporate, finance and real estate divisions? The contexts and the experience you will have gained are very different. Describing the organisation you worked for helps employers to understand your experience more easily.

Keep it brief Nobody has the time or inclination to read through extensive descriptions. You should be able to condense your experience into a few clear, concise points.

Focus on impact Simply listing duties undertaken is fine, but it's not particularly engaging. Where possible, focus on the impact you had in each role. Instead of saying you kept the clothes store neat at all times (a favourite on many a student CV), if you worked for a chain store with shop layout guidelines, you could say that you ensured that product layout consistently adhered to strict brand standards. Don't just say that you updated the company website; write about how you improved product information on the company website by extensively

My social media story: Justin Krutza – Technology Leader Programme at Target

I used social media to land my first job after graduation, even before starting a single class of my senior year. LinkedIn has been an integral part of my personal brand through online sources. When I was researching jobs and potential employers, LinkedIn was a great first start into discovering potential career paths and getting in contact with their recruiters.

While I was actively searching for full-time employment, I came across a job posting for a leadership programme within a large insurance company. LinkedIn helped me connect to the right people, and after a few messages back and forth, I secured a phone interview with someone who was in the programme. This happened without my applying through their website.

Just like how I used LinkedIn to find people, recruiters are constantly searching for potential employees. I've been contacted by recruiters representing Google and Cisco. Having a profile loaded with experiences, education and accomplishments increased my chances of being hired dramatically.

rewriting the web content, and simplified the text to enhance customers' understanding of the available product line.

The ability to work to targets is very important in a business context, so if you had targets that you met in any context, this is important information to include. This could be meeting and exceeding sales targets, or it could be something like "consistently produced monthly progress reports ahead of assigned deadlines". Obviously, only write this type of thing if you did it; never lie about what you've done or haven't done.

Make it meaningful Steer away from clichéd and empty sentences like "Improved my teamwork skills and worked effectively independently". This means nothing. Descriptions of skills are of no use if there is no evidence to back them up. If you are trying to communicate that you are good at working in teams, write about a time you did so successfully. If you want to show your ability to work independently, write about a project you managed alone. Avoid overused buzzwords like "hardworking", "passionate" and "motivated". If you're really passionate about something, give evidence of how you've engaged with the topic or sector to date. That's much more compelling than a generic statement with nothing to back it up.

Keep things professional This is not the place to list a job such as babysitting. You are trying to create the impression that you are a mature soon-to-be graduate, so focus on writing about experience that shows you in this light. Do list any part-time or casual work you have had, and do so in a way that shows transferable skills or emphasises that you are somebody who makes an impact wherever you go. The type of information that would be relevant to list here would be things like the following:

Retail Assistant, The Lemon Tree

The Lemon Tree is a busy newsagents beside Liverpool Street Station.

- Worked 12 hours per week while studying full time
- Processed up to 45 cash and card transactions per hour
- Devised a new lunchtime promotion and contributed to an 8 per cent increase in takings after one month

All of the above display skills – hard work and dedication, the ability to work quickly and an entrepreneurial attitude. These are things employers like to know. It can be hard to have an impact in a part-time role, but you if you stop and think back over any part-time jobs you have done, you might surprise yourself and come up with a few achievements or impacts which you could list in your profile.

Add media to your profiles

You can make your profile richer by including media in your "Summary", "Education" and "Experience" sections. The type of media you add could be a PDF of a project you carried out that is linked to the type of role you're targeting, a photograph that illustrates your experience, a video of you making a presentation or a link to your online portfolio if you have one. This type of media can help you to retain someone's attention on your profile and allows you to provide further evidence of your skills and abilities.

You also have the option of adding a background image to your profile. This will appear as a large banner image at the top of your page. It's not obligatory, but if you can find or upload an image that reflects the message you're trying to put across, it can be a good enhancement to your profile. These images usually do not include another photograph of the person, but tend to be graphics related to their profession.

Volunteer work, projects and languages

There are several other profile sections that you can fill in to create a comprehensive profile.

Volunteer work As mentioned earlier, you can include volunteer work in the experience part of your profile if it is more relevant to your sought-after job than your paid experience, or if you don't have much work experience to list. Alternatively, you can use this section to write about your volunteer work. It's great to be able to showcase your interests outside of coursework, and it takes commitment to juggle classes, assignments and volunteering, so this sends out the signal that you're good at managing multiple projects at the same time. This is a great selling point in the graduate job market.

Write about your voluntary activities in the same manner as you write about paid experience. Focus on impacts, achievements and any ways you can demonstrate your capabilities. Also, make sure to quantify what you do where possible, and to give a one- or two-line overview of the project for which you're volunteering. Here is an example of how you could write about voluntary experience.

Chapter 6

Friends of the Earth – Fundraising Volunteer

Friends of the Earth is a national charity which runs campaigns to raise public awareness regarding ways of combating climate change.

- Managed all aspects of setting up and running a table quiz on campus
- Negotiated free use of sports hall and seating and tables to accommodate 20 teams of five people
- Sold out the event through extensive promotion via email, Twitter and Facebook page
- Managed a team of seven volunteers who assisted with venue set-up, ticket selling and prize distribution
- Raised €800 on the night through ticket sales and donations

Projects The "Projects" section is a good place to highlight something important that you have done either in university or through work experience. You can include a project title as well as the completion date and detailed information about what exactly you did. As with everything else in your profile, you will want to include projects that show your skills and experience. If you are studying computer science and developed an app as part of your course, you could write about the process you used to develop and design it, and also outline the coding language you used to do so. If you are studying law and you took part in a moot court, you could write about the role that you played in this and the success that you had. These are just a few examples; the point is that any projects you participate in during university require you to develop and demonstrate skills. If you have limited work experience, outlining projects is an alternative way to make your LinkedIn profile more keyword-rich and to showcase your abilities.

Languages Language skills are a great asset. They can help businesses communicate with overseas suppliers, connect with international customers and expand into new markets. If you speak more than one language, this is something that can really impress employers, so make sure to add these to your LinkedIn profile. You can add them in your list of skills, but it's a good idea to also complete the "Languages" section of the profile.

As always, honesty is the best policy. If you can only say a few sentences in a second language that you picked up to get by on holiday, that won't get you very far in a business context, and it is probably best not to include it in your profile. However, if you've attended courses and feel that you can hold a conversation that goes beyond "Where is the train station?" and "What time is it?", then consider listing this in your profile. LinkedIn asks you to rate your skill level for every language you include. Their rating scale starts at elementary proficiency and goes all the way up to native or bilingual proficiency. Be honest in your assessment of your skills, so you don't get caught out, but if you do have some level of language skill, it's worth including this information in your profile.

A couple of other things

Follow news and influencers You can follow LinkedIn's news channels, and also follow LinkedIn influencers who post articles. Your profile will list the channels and people that you follow, so this provides another way for you to keep up to date and also to show that you are serious about your career interests. Channels include "Banking and Finance" "Big Data", "Healthcare", "Oil & Energy", "Logistics and Supply Chain", and so many more. There is an ever-growing range of news channels, so check in regularly to the "Customize News" option to see what's there.

Personalise your URL When you create an account, LinkedIn assigns a URL to your profile which is a random combination of letters and numbers. You can change this to create something much more visually appealing and succinct which is then easy to include in your email signature or on your CV. Go to the settings page, choose the option to edit your public profile, and then click on "Your public profile URL". Edit this so that your LinkedIn profile link now reads linkedin.com/in/yourname. There is a limit of 30 characters here, so if your name is long, you may have to be creative. You can change this up to five times every 180 days, but it's probably best to pick one and stick with it from then onwards. If you keep changing it, you might forget to change it in other places where you are cross-promoting it, and you don't want people clicking on a URL to nowhere. This is particularly important if you have a name shared by a lot of other people. If someone searching for you finds 20 Sarah Smiths, it will take them time to figure out which one is you. Make it easy by having a customised and consistent LinkedIn address.

Connect with people

LinkedIn is based around the value of connections: the value of staying connected to people you've met, and the value of being able to make new connections. Your LinkedIn profile is not an island; it should be one piece of a network. In order to achieve an All-Star profile, you need at least 50 connections, and you can build these up right away by connecting with people you already know who are on LinkedIn. If you have linked your address book with your LinkedIn account, you will be given a list of people you may know and want to connect with based on this.

The list of people you may know will show you their photograph if they have one, their name and their headline. There will also be a "Connect" button beside each name. Don't click that. It will automatically send a standard connection request, which is impersonal. Instead, click on the person's name, and this will bring you through to their profile. Once on the profile page, you can click the "Connect" button, and you will be given the option to personalise the message. It only takes a minute to do this, and it's important to do as it makes the connection a meaningful interaction, as opposed to an impersonal one.

Connecting with people you don't know

Connecting with people you already know, and know well, is the easy bit. Connecting with people you don't know as well, or at all, is the part that can seem difficult, but it's part of what makes LinkedIn so interesting. LinkedIn makes it easy to reach people, and you can connect with companies, recruiters and other people who could have an impact on your job search. Although you may be tempted to ignore the advice above about personalising your connection requests to people you know, do not, under any circumstances, send the standard connection request to people you don't know well. It comes across as lazy, and if you don't know the person and don't give her a reason why you want to connect, she is likely to ignore your request.

The answer to how you should approach somebody you don't know on LinkedIn comes down to knowing why you want to connect with her. When you find a recruiter who advertises jobs you think you would like to apply for, send her a connection request stating that you have noticed her posting a number of vacancies which you feel match your profile and that you would like to connect.

If you find someone who is working in a job you would love to do, and you would like to ask him for some advice, tell him. It's really not complicated, and it all comes back to the basic principles of networking discussed in Chapter 5. Explain why you are contacting the person, be enthusiastic, be polite and remember not to ask for a job.

You only have 300 characters to play with in a LinkedIn connection request. This is tight, but does leave room for key elements like a greeting, a brief outline of why you are interested in the person and an even briefer explanation of who you are. Don't make the request all about you and what you want to get. Make it about the person you are contacting. If you are contacting her because you came across her profile while researching careers and you found it really interesting, or you read an article she wrote on a website you like and you thought it was great, write that in your connection request. Here are a couple of examples to show you what a good connection request looks like.

Hello Emma,

I came across your profile while researching SOAS alumni working in India. I read about the work you're doing in the ICRC. It sounds so interesting. I would love to connect with you and hopefully find out a bit more about how you got to where you are today.

Thank you for your time,
David Power

Hello Peter,

I attended your workshop at the Grad Careers fair last week and found it really useful. I'm putting together my application to your firm at the moment, and you made it seem like a great place to work. I would like to connect with you here to read any insights that you share on LinkedIn.

Kind regards,
Fiona Harrison

Recommendations

Recommendations can be a great addition to your profile. When you have some work or voluntary experience, you could connect with your former manager and colleagues on LinkedIn. If you did a good job, you could consider asking them for recommendations. These are like reference letters for a job, except everybody can see them. Writing about all your skills and achievements is good, but getting a third party to confirm that you are as good as you say you are can create an even more positive impression.

You don't need to have a large number of recommendations. People have short attention spans, so it's better to have two or three great recommendations that will get read than ten recommendations that just seem like they'll take too long to read. One or two recommendations from former bosses would work well to further cement the good impression you are working to create online. Don't ask classmates to write recommendations for you. Everyone who looks at your profile can see who the person is that is recommending you, and that will not hold a lot of weight – it will just make you look like you are scraping the barrel somewhat.

To ask someone for a recommendation, go to the "Recommendation" section of your profile, and follow the prompts. LinkedIn will ask you to indicate which role you want a recommendation for, who you want to ask and how you are linked to that person – if you reported directly to him, for example – and then will show you a standard recommendation request. You can, and should, edit the standard recommendation request. When you ask for a recommendation, you are asking for somebody to take time out of his day to help you. Therefore, it's best to think about what skills or achievements you want him to highlight and make this clear in your initial request, to save everybody time and make the experience as pain-free as possible for all involved.

For example, if you are applying for roles where your ability to understand what a customer wants, and your tendency to pull out all the stops to deliver that, is important, you could ask the person if she could write about that. The text she writes will be emailed to you. You then have the option to accept the recommendation or you could go back to the person and ask for a few changes. You can also decide at any stage whether to share this recommendation on your profile for others to see.

Depending on how well you know the person, you might not feel entirely comfortable sending a recommendation request out of the blue. Another way to approach this is to send her an email or a message via LinkedIn and mention your request within that message. Then, if she says she is happy to recommend you, you could go through the formal process listed above.

When you are clear about what you want to be recommended for, and when your profile is complete, contact the people you have listed above with a tailored recommendation request.

Skills and endorsements

You can select a list of skills to include on your profile in the "Skills & Endorsements" section. Once you have done this, people to whom you are connected can endorse you for one or more of these skills

Exercise: Asking for a recommendation

Can you think of anybody you have reported to whom you could ask for a reference? Write down the name of one person, or two people if you can think of two, whom you could approach for a recommendation on LinkedIn. Then indicate what specifically you would like this person to recommend about you. Is it a particular task you accomplished, a specific skill you demonstrated or a more general recommendation?

	Name	Focus of recommendation
Person 1		
Person 2		

by the click of a button when they visit your profile. Endorsements are somewhat questionable because anybody can endorse you for anything without having any idea if you're actually good at what you say you are good at doing. However, they can be useful over time as, if you have a large number of endorsements for a particular set of skills, this gives a quick visual indicator to anybody reading your profile that you are probably good at the skills for which you are receiving endorsements. It's very much open to manipulation, but it can serve as an approximate indicator of your skill set.

What can sometimes happen is that your connections might be very aware of some of your skills, but not aware of others. You might have listed 20 skills but could find that people are regularly endorsing you for a small number of these which are not core to the brand you want to present. LinkedIn lists your skills in descending order, starting at the top with the one for which you have received the most endorsements. This means skills you want to highlight may get pushed to the bottom of the list, and people probably won't take the time to look that far down. LinkedIn allows you to manually edit this section, so you can move your key skills to the top of the list. This will make them more visible and hopefully prompt endorsements for those skills when people look at your profile from then onwards.

Endorse honestly When you are considering endorsing someone, it's best only to do so if you have first-hand knowledge of the individual's skill. If you have seen this person in action using a particular skill, it's fine to give an endorsement. For example, if you have connected with a marketing director who spoke at a careers event in your university, you could endorse him for public speaking because you have witnessed that, so that would be completely appropriate. However it would be a bit unusual to endorse him for search engine optimisation if you don't actually know first-hand that he does this well. Stick to this approach and you can come to the attention of people by endorsing them in a genuine manner, thus creating a positive impression.

Finding and applying for jobs

You can find vacancies on LinkedIn by clicking on the "Jobs" tab. When you click on this, LinkedIn will list a range of "Jobs you may be interested in". This list of suggested jobs is generated based upon the information you have provided in your profile. To edit the types of jobs shown here, change your preferred location, company size and industry on the jobs page. You can search for jobs on LinkedIn similarly to any other jobs board, by putting in your career key words to find suitable vacancies.

Another feature of the jobs page is that it will show you vacancies in companies to which you are connected through your network. Scroll down the "Jobs" page to "Discover jobs in your network" to see companies that are hiring to which you have some connection. You can also narrow down your search to graduate vacancies by going directly to https://www.linkedin.com/studentjobs and filtering the results by industry and location.

When you identify and click on a job to which you would like to apply, there will be a blue button under the job title which will either say "Apply on company website", or "Apply now". If the option is to apply on the company's website, click the button and you will be redirected to the vacancy on the company's own webpage, and you can follow the instructions to apply from there.

If the option on LinkedIn is "Apply now", a pop up window will give you the option of editing the email address to which a response will be sent, editing your phone number, and uploading documents. If you apply through LinkedIn the recruiter will then be able to see your profile, but it's still worth taking the option to upload your tailored CV and a cover letter at this stage. Your LinkedIn profile can be difficult to tailor to a role if you are applying for numerous positions. Therefore attaching a more targeted CV could help you to demonstrate your suitability for the role.

LinkedIn groups

Groups are a great feature, and they serve multiple purposes. They allow you to join communities of people like you or people doing the things you would like to do. Active groups also provide useful information and inspiration about what the latest industry news is in different sectors.

By joining groups that are linked to your career interests, you will add further evidence of your serious search for work. You can choose to display the groups of which you are a member on your profile, so this is another way of confirming your professional aspirations to any readers. You will also be able to raise your profile by sharing useful articles and liking and commenting on other people's posts to the group page. Don't ever spam a group by posting self-promoting posts or material that is not relevant to the group in the hope of gaining attention. It is unprofessional and will alienate group members, which could include potential employers.

You can find groups by clicking on "Interests" and then on "Groups". LinkedIn will suggest some groups to you based on the keywords it scans in your profile, and you can search for more. Many groups are private, meaning you'll have to get permission to join. Once you click the "Join" button, the group administrator will view your profile and determine if you are a good fit.

When you decide to join groups, do your research and choose groups that are aligned with your career aspirations. This is another way of emphasising the type of roles you are genuinely interested in attaining. For example, if you're looking for a job where your multilingual skills are front and centre, you might want to join groups like these:

- Language jobs
- Language network
- Leaders in foreign language.

It's also a good idea to join any LinkedIn groups that are related to your education, such as your university's alumni group or groups for current and past students of your course. This immediately connects you with a network of people who not only come from the same background as you but could very well be working in jobs that you might like to find out more about.

Participating in groups

Groups are a fantastic source of information, but they are also a space where you can grow your visibility by participating. There are various ways to interact with a group, and you can start off slowly and then take part more once your confidence with LinkedIn increases.

Basic level You can start with the very light touch interaction of clicking "Like" on someone's post or comment. This is a simple way to get your toe in the water. When you "like" someone's post, she will receive an alert to tell her this, and that could lead to her checking out your profile, so it's a simple tool to use if you're trying to get on the radar of someone in a group, with a view to connecting with this person to ask for advice.

Intermediate level The next step up in participating is commenting on people's posts. If somebody has written an article that you like, you could write a comment stating what particularly stood out to you in what he said. Or if a debate ensues in the comments, as often occurs in these forums, you could get involved and share your views. The usual rules for social media interactions apply here: don't write anything if you have nothing to say, and keep things polite. A very basic comment could be as simple as "This is really useful advice – thank you", and this is fine if you are just trying to come to someone's attention. A more thoughtful comment would be something along the lines of "I really enjoyed this post, and I agree with what you've said about the value of getting your foot in the door of a company even if the job itself isn't ideal. I started in an administrative role in a research laboratory during my summer holidays, and I feel this puts me in a better position to get a research assistant role when I graduate."

Advanced If you want to take your interactions a step further, you can initiate discussions in a group. You could ask the group a question or share an article that is relevant to the group's focus.

If you're asking a question, make sure it's one that would be interesting to a number of readers, so don't make it all about you. It would be better to ask "What do you think new graduates need to have on their CV to be successful in applying for a management consulting role?" rather than "I have some experience working part-time in a large store, and was an active member of my university's investment society. Do you think this qualifies me for a job in investment?" This question is all about you, and it's a little bit of a stretch to ask a group of people you don't know for personalised career advice. The former question, however, is not specific to you, and any answers people provide would be useful to other group members who are at the beginning of their careers.

What to do next

If you feel you have a good handle on LinkedIn, move on to the next chapters about other social media sites. If you'd like to start using it to network but want to read up on how to network effectively, go to Chapter 5 on making career connections.

Chapter 6

Useful websites

www.lindseypollak.com Lindsey Pollak is the author of one of Forbes's "Top 100 websites for your career" and is a LinkedIn ambassador. She shares news about the latest developments via her social media channels.

https://help.linkedin.com LinkedIn's extremely comprehensive help pages have the answer to any question you could possibly have about using the site, and if they don't have the answer listed, you can ask a question in the forum.

https://university.linkedin.com/linkedin-for-students This is LinkedIn's information page aimed specifically at university students. Keep an eye on it to keep up to date with LinkedIn developments and to read tips for making the most out of the site.

Make the most of Twitter

Contents

Twitter has become a powerhouse in the social media world, attracting everyone from thought leaders to celebrities to the "average person", and everyone in between. It provides a fun and easy way to discover news and hear the latest updates from people you know and those you admire, as well as a way to interact with people who would otherwise be difficult to access. It's a great place to share your thoughts and experiences, and a brilliant place to research and interact with companies.

Overview

Twitter has a more "social" atmosphere than LinkedIn, and yet for the savvy job-hunter, it can provide valuable information and networking opportunities. There are entire communities of like-minded people – people in roles you would love – and they're regularly tweeting content related to their work. This is the place to find out what people are working on, to hear about trending topics in different sectors and to know what prominent people in the industry have to say about them. This makes Twitter a real gold mine when it comes to researching and understanding careers. It can also give your an edge when doing background research before you write a job application or attend an interview.

Twitter terms

Twitter has its own terminology, and you should familiarise yourself with this so that you can navigate the platform more easily. The glossary in the following table will give you an overview of the basic Twitter terms you need to know.

Twitter glossary	
Twitter handle	Your chosen name on Twitter, preceded by the "@" symbol e.g. @johnsmith or @javagirl
Tweet	Your posts on Twitter are called "tweets". They can be up to 140 characters long
# (hashtag)	# is the symbol attached to keywords in your tweet – for example, "Busy writing applications, trying to get this #career figured out for when I #graduate in June!" You can use hashtags to label the theme of your tweet, so if someone searches for tweets about #graduate, your tweet will come up in this search.
RT (retweet)	When you share someone else's tweet, this is called a "retweet". You can click the "Retweet" button to share the entire tweet, and this will also give you the option to preface it with your own tweet commenting on what you're sharing. When you use the "Retweet" function, the original poster will get an alert in his "notifications" tab.
MT (modified tweet)	If you want to manually share someone's tweet and incorporate it into your own tweet, you'll probably need to edit down the original tweet so that it all fits in 140 characters. Preface the modified tweet with "MT" to indicate that you've edited it, for example "Great tip to make sure you send those CVs and cover letters in on time. MT @careertips Make a job application schedule and stick to it". When you share someone's tweet in this way, she will receive a notification in her "Mentions" tab because you will have mentioned her Twitter handle in your own tweet.
Favourite	You might see a tweet that you like and that you want to refer to later. Clicking the "Favourite" button will alert the person who shared it that you've liked it, and you will be able to find that tweet later in you "Favourites" tab.

Your profile

Now that you have a basic idea of Twitter language, your next step is to create your profile.

Simple set-up

Signing up on Twitter is as simple as registering with an email address and a password. You choose a username and can upload a profile picture. You're then ready to follow and interact with around one billion people and company accounts on the platform.

Your profile picture

Twitter is a social, largely informal platform, and you can reflect this with the photograph you use for your profile.

As with all social media, the emphasis is on giving people a sense of who you are, so it's better to include a profile photo that shows your face instead of an inanimate object or a sunset. The photo doesn't need to be formal or professional; as long as you avoid the obvious no-nos, such as photos showing a little too much skin or a picture of you doing something you wouldn't want your granny to see, you should be fine.

Your Twitter "bio"

You have 160 characters to write a few words about yourself, and this information will show up on your profile. You can personalise this by saying who you are, what you're interested in and what you tweet about. In addition, you can include links to any other profiles you have online.

Go back to the keywords exercise, and pick two or three things that you want to communicate in your brief Twitter bio. Although Twitter is relaxed, remember that you're still connecting with potential employers, so it's a good idea to include skills and keywords here. It's okay to include a bit of humour as this shows your personality.

Who to follow

One of the first things you'll want to do once you've set up your account is to begin following other Twitter users. You might want to follow people you know in your own life, people you admire and companies you hope might employ you. Twitter can be an extremely powerful tool to help you find potential employers and get an insight into the work that they do and their company culture. You should search for and follow a range of accounts:

- Follow companies in your sector of interest. You never know when they might have a job opportunity available.
- Follow individuals working at your target companies. See what topics are coming up in that sector, and get an insight into their working life.
- Follow companies and people who can help you produce a better CV through tips and helpful information.

If you're studying history and history of art, and would love to work in a museum or cultural centre, search for and follow museums in the geographical area you want to work in, but also further afield. Following some well-known museums internationally will show you have a broad outlook and a wide interest in the area, and this could also lead you to some interesting reads and inspiration.

Run a search on a search engine to find key people working in the sector, and if you can find them on Twitter, click "Follow". Companies and individuals often include their Twitter handles on their websites. As you start following people, go to their profiles, see whom they are following, quoting and retweeting, and consider following those people too. If you use this method, you'll find that you can very quickly create a long list of interesting accounts to follow. They in turn can give great insight into trending topics in your area of interest, help you to find out who the thought leaders are and inform you when jobs you might like to apply for are advertised.

There are plenty of Twitter accounts dedicated to posting jobs. Follow general job site accounts like @graduatejobsUK or @guardian_jobs to get a sense of what's out there. You could also follow accounts that tweet jobs related to specific sectors. There are countless Twitter accounts which are very tailored to different careers, such as @polscijobs, @PsychJobs and @animationjobs. Simply run a keyword search for your desired job title and location, along with the word "job", to locate accounts relevant to you. For example, you could search for "PR Edinburgh jobs" and find a list of Twitter accounts posting interesting roles. This is a way not only to find vacancies but also to see what types of roles most frequently come up and what these organisations look for, which is useful information when you're deciding what options are open to you.

My social media story: Sarah Bermingham, Journalist, Storyful

When I discovered Twitter, I learnt over time how to set up my timeline in such a way that it kept me up to date with events and news stories happening nationally and internationally, and created the illusion for me (even if this was slightly exaggerated) that I was connected with journalists by being able to follow and interact with them. This strengthened my confidence that I could also join that world. I think Twitter is a particularly brilliant platform for young journalists, to this end.

I was also able to use social media quite effectively while at third level in the course of my duties with the college newspaper. I sourced stories through tracing people's digital footprint, and this ultimately helped me land a job in social media journalism. As a result of that journalism experience at third level, I was lucky enough to win a National Student Media Award. On foot of that, I was approached by an editor at Storyful News Agency via the social media platform Twitter, enquiring as to whether I'd be interested in completing an internship. The skills, experience and attitude I had fostered through growing up using a variety of social media for a variety of purposes helped me land the role. I'm now working there full-time, curating and using social media and loving it.

Hashtags

The # hashtag symbol is Twitter's way of categorising tweets according to themes. You will see the # symbol as you scroll through people's tweets, usually beside a keyword or phrase. By clicking any of them, for example #devchat or #codingnews or #chemjobs, you can quickly gain access to an extremely targeted feed of information that is of specific interest to you.

Exercise: Find a hashtag and related tweets

There are many websites where you can put in your keywords and find related hashtags.

1. Go to www.twubs.com and search for one of your career keywords in the search function, or look through the list of highlighted hashtags to see what is of interest.
2. Put the hashtag you're interested in into the search bar on Twitter to see what people are tweeting on the subject.
3. Twitter automatically shows you the "Top tweets" with this hashtag. Click "All tweets" to access even more related updates.

Hashtags are a great way to draw attention to your tweets. It can be helpful to run a keyword search in a search engine to find out what popular hashtags are being used. For example, if you're an aspiring writer, you could search for "hashtags writing", and you will find a list of popular hashtags relating to writing. When you incorporate one or several of these into your own tweets, other people who are searching for that hashtag will also see your tweets. This can be a great way of connecting with like-minded people and building up your Twitter community.

Twitter chats

Twitter chats are Twitter "events" where a group of like-minded individuals use a hashtag that has been pre-agreed and have an online conversation about their thoughts or experiences in relation to that topic. This might include chatting about a conference, a current affairs story or careers advice related to different sectors.

Career-related chats are often led by organisations. They may be hiring and hence researching who is out there, or they may simply be trying to drum up interest in their business. Either way, taking part in these will improve your exposure in that specific business category.

Search for and participate in Twitter chats that make the most sense to you. If your interest lies in fashion, contribute frequently to Twitter chats about fashion week or the launch of a new collection by a

Chapter 7

Employer's View: Ashley Hever, Talent Acquisition Manager UK & Ireland at Enterprise Rent-A-Car

It almost goes without saying that if you're job hunting, it is always a good idea to follow and converse on social media with the companies you might want to work with. This will help you to develop a strong understanding of the industry you're interested in and the key companies in the arena, which will in turn help you to decide where you want to work and what you could contribute to the field. At Enterprise we engage with candidates in this way on a regular basis and tools such as Twitter make up a huge part of the recruitment process."

designer you admire. If environmental science is your interest, tweet about an ongoing energy crisis summit or recently released climate change research. There are several online databases where you can search for upcoming Twitter chats, such as www.tweetreports.com. You will find Twitter chats covering a wide range of job search and career-related topics such as #DigiJobsHour (advice on jobs in the digital industry), #InternPro (advice on securing an internship) and #SportJC (jobs in sports). The date and time of these scheduled chats is listed alongside a description of the topic being covered.

Conferences often have hashtags associated with them, so if you run a search online for "conference" and your keywords, for example "Conference human resources" and include the current year as well, you should be able to find upcoming conferences. Go to their websites to see if they have listed a hashtag. On the days when the conference is running, search for that hashtag so you can follow events as delegates tweet about them and include the hashtag in their tweets.

Taking control of Twitter

List logic

Twitter can get a little addictive once you get the hang of it. If you do become hooked, you might find that keeping track of all the people you follow becomes difficult. You might also discover that you're following people in lots of different walks of life. For example, you could be following numerous universities if you want to work in academia, and you could also be following your favourite interior designers or travel-writing tweeters. Sometimes you'll only be interested in reading tweets to do with your job search, and sometimes you'll want to block those out and read more entertaining content.

To keep track of those you follow and make it easier to only read what you want to on a given day, create lists of Twitter accounts according to categories. You could have a "foodie" list, a "think tanks" list, a "career advice" list and so on.

You don't have to categorise everyone you follow, but the more you do this, the more you can tailor your own Twitter experience. It is also a handy way for anyone looking at your profile to see what your main interests are much more quickly than trawling through the whole list of people you follow.

Another advantage of lists is that when you add someone to a list, he will get an alert notifying him of this, so it can be another way to come to someone's attention. With that in mind, think about what you name your list – someone is more likely to be flattered and look at your profile if she receives an alert saying she's been added to your "International development leaders" list rather than "Random dev people", for example.

Your tweets

Your Twitter feed is, by default, publicly accessible. There is an option to protect your tweets so that only people you specifically allow to do so can read your tweets, but there's probably not much point tweeting if you're keeping it all under wraps. You might opt not to tweet at all, but just to use Twitter to follow accounts that provide helpful information for your job search and to look for vacancies. If you do decide to tweet, fill your Twitter feed with a wide variety of content, from your own thoughts, ideas and photographs of interesting things you come across, to engaging content from around the web. It can take a bit of practice to be able to get a message across in just 140 characters, but it can be done.

If you are sharing links, these can take up a lot of space. You can use a link-shortening website like https://bitly.com to convert a long web address into a short code that you can include in your tweet. It's free to use and gives you more space to write what you want to say about the link you're sharing.

Keep your brand and your target industries in mind as you tweet. You want to aim for a mix of career-focused and personal tweeting, to show your focus but also to let readers get to know you a little bit at the same time. For example, if you want to let people know you have great leadership skills, you could tweet about the sports team you captain, or a group project that you led that went well. You could demonstrate time management by tweeting about getting three essays in on time in one week while working 10 hours in a café. You could show that you are interested in community work by tweeting about your volunteering activities. The range is endless.

Interacting on Twitter

You can interact with people on Twitter in a number of ways. Following them is not really interacting – it's just a basic first step. You can "favourite" people's tweets that you like, or reply directly to tweets that others have written. Bear in mind that those replies can be seen by anyone who clicks through that person's profile, so keep the golden rules of social media interaction in mind at all times. Another way to interact with people is to tag them in your tweets by including their Twitter handle. For example, if you went to a talk by a guest lecturer and you wanted to tweet some of his insights, you could find his Twitter handle, if he has one, and tweet quotes from the speech, with the speaker's handle included. This way he will get an alert to say you have mentioned him on Twitter, so it's a simple way of acknowledging the person. He might even retweet what you have posted, gaining you a few more followers.

It's not just individuals who are active on Twitter. An increasing number of graduate recruiters are using Twitter to build their brand and interact with students. Check Twitter feeds of companies you're targeting, to see what opportunities there are to interact. Many companies have specific career accounts on Twitter, and some also run separate accounts specifically to promote their graduate opportunities. A company might tweet something like "Our new #graduate #careers page is live. Let us know what you think #companyxgradcareers". You could respond to this tweet, saying something like "The new site is great – so much useful information about the different areas of work I could go into", or you could tweet, "Really liking @companyxgradcareers new #gradcareers page, now I just need to get my CV sorted…"

Most employers are not looking for social media "stars" to work for them, so don't be overly concerned with building a large number of followers. If you do have an active account, aim to share tweets that demonstrate your brand to any prospective employer who might take a look at your profile. Showcasing your ability to create a strong online brand for yourself can go a long way towards a recruiter seeing you as someone who knows what they want and knows how to leverage social media to market themselves. This can improve your chances of coming across as a serious candidate who would be a valuable asset to their organisation.

Build your presence

The inclination of many first-time Twitter users is to rack up as many followers as possible, in the hopes that if each new follower "follows back", they will be "popular" in no time. Twitter is not a popularity contest, and you're not likely to lose a potential job because you don't have a large Twitter following – unless you're going for a social media marketing role, in which case, building a strong following here can be a great way to showcase your skills.

It's possible to buy followers, and there are many websites offering this option. It's not a great idea to go down this route, as anyone taking more than a cursory glance through your account will quickly see that these accounts are not real. If someone can work this out, you run the risk of appearing untrustworthy and deceitful – neither of which are the attributes of a great graduate hire. A Twitter account with a high number of followers but little activity will sound an alarm bell for anyone familiar with the platform. It's not ethical and it will give you a very bad image.

If you are interested in building your follower base, it's much better to have a small but loyal and interactive set of followers that you have gained by being active on Twitter in a thoughtful and interesting manner. Follow interesting people and retweet the tweets that made you think. Tweets with media get more clicks, so share photos and videos in your tweets. Post tweets where you tag other accounts if the updates you're sharing would be interesting to them. This can all help you to grow your number of followers in a more organic manner.

What to do next

Spend some time playing around with Twitter and all its features. If you're clear on how to use it, move on to Chapters 8 and 9 to learn about other social media sites that can also help your job search. If you're not sure about what to say online, go back to Chapters 2 and 3 to review what you have to offer and how to build your brand online.

Useful websites

www.wefollow.com This website makes it easy to find people to follow on social media. Enter your keywords into the search bar on the home page, and you will be given a list of prominent people who talk about those keywords on social media.

https://tagdef.com/ If you're seeing a hashtag coming up in your newsfeed and you're not sure what it's about, go to this site, search for the hashtag and you will find a definition telling you what it's all about.

Make the most of blogging

Contents

A blog is an online platform that you control, where you can publish posts about topics of interest to you. Bloggers do everything from reviewing books, movies and fashion lines to posting thoughtful analyses of developments in their area of interest, and so much more. Blogs are a uniquely personal collection of reflections and ideas where the writer shares her thoughts and opinions.

Overview

If you want greater freedom and independence when managing your online profile, blogging is the answer. Writing your own blog is a great way to showcase your interest in a career area. It can also be about any topic that you're really interested in, and it doesn't have to be career-focused. The mere act of regularly sharing well-crafted blog posts is an excellent way of showing how you consistently manage an extracurricular project. Blogging takes thought and time, and it requires a range of highly transferable skills, including writing, design and, if you work hard to successfully promote your blog, social media marketing. It also displays a level of confidence, as it can be hard to put yourself out there online and express your world view. Taking the time to keep abreast of developments in your area of interest, and to share your thoughts on these, can make you stand out from other candidates.

Blogs can cover a wide range of themes. Topics you might consider blogging about include the ones listed here:

- Student life
- Your view of local or international current affairs
- Reviews of books you read
- Your travels
- A blog co-written with other students about the highs and lows of setting up and running a start-up company together.

Exercise: What could you write about?

Is there something you're really interested in that you would consider blogging about? Think about the websites you always end up on, the conversation topics you frequently return to, the parts of your course you spend the most time engaging with. If anything jumps out, jot it down in the box below.

Possible blog topics:

If nothing springs to mind right away, don't immediately decide that blogging isn't for you. If the idea of blogging appeals, stay alert to the topics that interest you most and revisit this advice if an idea for a blog occurs to you at a later date. Read on to find out more about blogging and see if it sounds like something you would like to invest time in doing well.

Lurk before you leap

Before you start blogging, run a keyword search and take a look at the blogs that are already out there related to the topic you're considering writing about. What do you like about these blogs? What would you do differently? If you're not already following a few blogs and aren't sure where to start, a quick search for your career keywords and "blog" should result in some interesting suggestions.

Writing a great blog

Write in your own style

Make your blog unique by writing in your own voice and using your own style. Your personal perspective is what makes your blog interesting. Remember that the key thing to keep in mind when blogging to enhance your online brand is to create content that reflects your interests, skills, career values and personality. Your blog doesn't have to be the most original, unique or popular for these purposes. It just needs to provide evidence to any employer who reads it that you are genuinely interested in a topic, that you have good writing skills and that you have the drive to keep a side project like a blog up to date while balancing your other commitments.

Words and pictures

Photographs typically accompany news stories and magazine articles. They catch your eye and can make someone decide to continue reading. Try to use graphics, images or videos that complement your words and make your blog appealing to readers. You can upload your own images or share images from other sites. Flickr.com's "Creative Commons" filter is where you can find images that photographers allow others to use. There are different levels of permission to share, so always check these. Wherever you find the images you want to use, make sure to always credit the source.

Content is king

Blogging is about creating content. Every post you write, every poll you post, every reaction you make and even the shared pieces that you gather from other websites – video clips, fashion layouts, thought pieces, recipes, and so on – are a form of content. What makes content so special is that it is unique to the content creator: you. Keep in mind the online brand you want to create for yourself – academic, professional, creative, thoughtful – and strive to deliver content that closely aligns both with you as a potential employee, as well as with the companies you want to work for. What content do they create? What would impress them?

Engage your readers

Engaging content is content that actively invites readers to participate, respond, think or otherwise become engaged with what you've written. A current news story followed by your reactions and an invitation to readers to share their views; a post in which you present three alternative book covers or layouts or fashion designs, and invite readers to "vote" for their favourite; a poll; or a Q&A – these can all make your blog more accessible and interesting to readers.

Getting started

Your blog name

Naming your blog is something you should invest time into doing. You could simply use your name so that anybody searching for you will quickly spot it in a search for your name online. You could include a keyword so it's easily found, like "Architect at work" or "Literary Musings". Or you could go for something more creative or playful that reflects your personality and your subject. Whatever name you choose for your blog, keep it short; people are more likely to remember a simple, brief name than something long and complicated. When you have a name or two in mind, put them into a search engine to check that they're not already taken.

Free blog or paid?

You can choose to set up a blog for free by having it hosted on the main blogging platforms like Wordpress or Blogger. There are a number of limitations that come with a free hosted blog. When you choose your blog name, the hosting service's name will be included in your blog title, for example "yourblog.wordpress.com". The other issue is that you won't actually have any rights over the name of your blog, called your blog domain, so technically your blog could be shut down or the name could be reassigned to someone else, and this would be outside of your control. Your access to different design themes will be limited, and there is also a limit on the amount of space you can use, which means you won't be able to post an unlimited number of large files such as photographs or videos. If you don't want to include a lot of images and don't mind not having a lot of customisation options available, a free blog can work for your purposes.

The paid route gives you more control and more options. You can buy the domain name you want on websites which register domain names, such as GoDaddy, Namecheap or Gandi. You will then own that domain name for the term of the contract – this usually lasts a year and can then be renewed. You will also have a much larger range of free design themes to choose from make your blog look the way you want it to appear. You will also get access to more customisation elements such as plug-ins which can make your blog more user-friendly. In addition to paying for your domain name, you'll have to pay a website to host your blog. This usually involves a small monthly fee. Some hosting sites offer free domain name registration when you pay for hosting. Once you have bought your domain and set up an account with a hosting site, you can then download Wordpress's software onto your blog and take advantage of all the features it offers to personalise your blog.

Plan your content

Writing a content calendar, where you map out what you want to post about week by week, can help you stay on top of your posts and provide inspiration. You completed a sample content calendar covering all your social media channels in the first chapter. Blogging requires a content calendar of its own. This helps to keep momentum going and counter "writer's block". You might find that one week you're "in the zone" and can write a few posts, whereas other weeks you don't feel as inspired. Keeping a content calendar can help you store those "extra" posts and ideas for content, and help you remember to post them at regular intervals. This can sustain you through the inevitable times when you suffer from writer's block while trying to keep your blog updated.

A content calendar for your first few posts could look something like this:

Chapter 8

Sample blog schedule	
Blog title: Working Language: A blog about careers with languages	
Week 1	Welcome post – outline who I am and blog themes
Week 2	"Who's hiring?" A post about graduate roles where language skills are a job requirement

Week 3	"Top ten sites for your multilingual job search" A well-researched list of local and international web pages that advertise vacancies for linguists
Week 4	"My linguist life": Introducing "My linguist life" series, monthly interview carried out with someone working in a career with languages
Week 5	"Let your languages do the talking": How to highlight language skills in job applications

If you came up with some ideas for blog topics earlier in this chapter, use the following blank blog schedule to sketch out your idea in more detail, and see if this is something you think could really work as an online branding tool for you.

Exercise: Your sample blog schedule

Jot down your ideas for blog posts around your core blog idea in the following table.

Blog subjects	
Week 1	
Week 2	
Week 3	
Week 4	
Week 5	
Week 6	
Week 7	

If you found it difficult to come up with lots of ideas, don't let that switch you off the idea of blogging just yet. Do a bit of online research, see what other people who blog about your proposed topic are doing and see if you feel a bit more inspired. Sometimes it's just getting started that can be the hard part, so take your time exploring other blogs and gathering ideas.

As you can see, there is more to blogging than simply posting a few thoughts online once a month and then letting your blog gather dust. If blogging seems like too much work, but there's something you're really interested in, why not sit down with others who share that interest and set up a blog together, taking turns posting new content? This will provide anyone looking you up online with content you have written, and it will be interesting to employers. If you're stuck for examples of teamwork at an interview, this could be a good one to use.

Your posts

Your first post should set the scene. You may have spent a lot of time planning what to blog about, but you need to make it clear from the outset what your blog is going to be focusing on. Tell readers who you are, why you're writing about your chosen topic and what your plans are for the blog. Consider drafting a few posts before you even set up your blog, to see if you enjoy the process and if you have enough to say. If you're feeling nervous about posting, you could always get a friend or two to cast an eye over your post before you hit "Publish". After that, it's simply a matter of getting to grips with the different design options and playing around with the post until you're happy with how it looks. You can preview posts so that you know exactly what they will look like before you hit "Publish".

Turn up the volume

New bloggers may find blogging frustrating because they seem to be "shouting into a vacuum", and it can be de-motivating when you work hard on crafting a post only to feel like it's drifting like a lone piece of tumbleweed across the expanse of the Internet. Simply writing posts, no matter how brilliant, is not enough to draw readers to your blog. If you want to drive traffic to your blog, you'll need to create a little bit of noise about what you're doing.

Chapter 8

Let your network know that you are writing. Share a status update about it on Facebook, and include a "call to action". In other words, don't just say, "Here's my blog"; say something like, "Here's my new blog about x. Check it out and share it with your friends". You could go a step further and set up a Facebook page specifically for your blog, with the same name. You could use that to share blog links and gather and interact with followers. Tweet about it too, and consider listing your blog name in your email signature if your blog is professionally focused.

Share your blog posts regularly on your other social media sites like Facebook, Twitter and LinkedIn. Only share on LinkedIn if the blog is related to a professional sector you are actively targeting. As you grow your own blog, you can make a habit of regularly visiting other blogs in your field of interest, and explore these also. Find a handful you like – less is more, in this case – and comment regularly on posts that genuinely interest or excite you. Become a regular presence and, chances are, that blogger and his followers will take a look at your blog as well.

Some bloggers who are trying to build traffic posts comment by saying things like "This post is great, and I have written a similar one that you might enjoy – here's a link". This is probably not the ideal approach, as it seems they are only commenting for self-serving purposes. Make comments that contribute to the discussion and let your words entice people to click on your name, which will lead them to your blog.

Blogging can seem intimidating. All those words, all that time and energy, all that work and potentially all those people reading what you have to say. If something really interests you, why not try it and see how you fare? You might find that you're quite good at it, and it can be a very enjoyable and rewarding project which has the added bonus of demonstrating a range of skills to employers who look you up online.

What to do next

If you like the sound of blogging and have an idea or two for a blog subject, sit down and think about what subject you could write about in a sustained manner over a series of posts. Then try drafting a content calendar to see if you have a few ideas for content. If you want to find out about less time-intensive social media sites, the next chapter will take you through Facebook, Pinterest and Instagram.

Useful websites

www.bloggingbasics101.com This website gives you a wealth of great information on how to set up and manage a blog from scratch.

www.startbloggingonline.com This website includes step-by-step guides on getting your blog up and running and has useful advice and tips.

Chapter **9**

Make the most of Facebook, Pinterest, Instagram and Video CVs

Contents

Facebook, Pinterest and Instagram might not be central to your job search, but they can play a strong supporting role. Video CVs, though not social media per se, are a dynamic medium for communicating your brand and can be easily shared across your social media profiles. This chapter will take you through how each of these platforms can help with your job-seeking efforts.

Facebook

Facebook is one of the longest-running and most popular social media platforms in existence, with over 1.44 billion monthly active users.[12] Since its inception, members have mostly used it as a medium for staying in touch with their friends, but is becoming increasingly relevant for jobseekers, with apps being developed to help companies create more engaging business pages where readers can learn about them, see their latest job postings and interact. Even if you're already present on Facebook, there are things you need to think about when you're job seeking, to make sure your Facebook presence is doing you justice.

Points for privacy

Privacy has already been discussed earlier in this guide, but it's impossible to place too much emphasis on the importance of keeping some things under lock and key. As Facebook is seen primarily as a purely social network, you may decide that you don't want it to play any role in your job search at this stage. That's absolutely fine, but even if this is the case, take a few minutes to secure your privacy settings on Facebook. It's possibly the biggest repository of any digital dirt you might have, so doing this is vital.

It can be time-consuming to go back through your posts, hiding messages that are perhaps a bit too "edgy" and untagging yourself from inappropriate photographs, but it's worth it to prevent anything potentially damaging from impacting negatively on your job prospects. The privacy settings on Facebook that matter the most include what we will look at next.

Choose your Facebook privacy settings

Almost everything you need to know about privacy settings is explained under the "Choose your privacy settings" tab, where you can allow some features and disable others, such as allowing access to your posts to "Everyone", "Friends of Friends", "Friends" or "Other". Key settings to adjust include the following:

What others can post on your wall In the "Timeline and tagging" section of your settings, you can opt to review posts friends tag you in before they appear on your timeline. This is a simple measure which gives you control over what appears on your profile.

Contact information You don't want everyone in the world to know your home phone number or address. However, it can be a good idea to share some contact information in case an employer is trying to get in touch with you. You could share a professional email address, your Twitter handle, blog address or LinkedIn profile URL. It goes without saying that the best type of email address when job searching is a simple one, which only includes your name.

Tagged photographs Numerous and legendary are the tales of "looks great on paper" jobseekers whose job prospects are derailed by a questionable Facebook photo. Clamping down on your settings can help eliminate this threat. Simply go to the main privacy page, click

"Customise Settings" and then scroll down to "Photos and videos I'm tagged in". From there, you can manually check who can see your photos and videos. Or to be on the safe side, customise the setting until it reads "Only me".

Information accessible through your friends Adjusting the settings in this section, located under the "Apps and Websites" tabs, will allow you to avoid letting posts and information from friends negatively affect what can be seen on your Facebook feed.

> ## My social media story: Rushyda Syed, Video Journalist, NRK Østlandssendingen
>
> I am currently working for NRK Østlandssendingen as an interning VJ (video journalist) as part of a recruitment program for multicultural journalists. I found the job on the company's website. I had an old acquaintance who was married to someone who had been in the program before, and I got in touch with him through Facebook, to ask his advice as to how I should proceed. He gave me advice as to how I should angle my application and what I should do, should I get called in for an interview. The information was invaluable, and I was called in for an interview and actually got the job.

Take it up a notch

Facebook is a very social site, but that doesn't mean it can't help you to find a job. Interacting with the growing number of companies who have Facebook pages can get you on their radar and keep you up to date with company news.

Interact with companies

Companies are investing time in building their own brands on this platform, and Facebook is creating new ways for them to promote themselves, such as adding a "Jobs" tab where they can share their current vacancies. Search for and "like" or "follow" company pages, or join Facebook pages that are in line with your industry or area of interest. When you choose to like or follow a particular page, not only are you showing them that you have an interest in their company, you also then have a running feed of material to like and share that is closely in line with the industry in which you would like to work. This can help to keep your career interests and job search on your Facebook friends' radars, increasing the chance that they will think of you if they hear of a relevant opportunity.

This isn't going to get you the job, but it will keep you up to date with what's happening in the company, and you can reference what you found interesting about its Facebook page at the interview, if they have done something particularly different or creative that caught your eye. All this can help you build evidence for the "Why do you want to work at our company?" question.

Broadcast your job search

Let people on Facebook know about your job search. You never know who might know somebody who does work at a company that you want to find out more about. The people you are connected to on Facebook are your friends, so they are likely to want to help you if they can. You could post a status update simply saying, "I'd love to talk to somebody working in event management. Does anybody out there know anyone in that line of work?" The tone is casual, as you are speaking to your friends, so don't worry too much about being overly formal. Your friends are your allies, so don't be afraid to ask; you might be surprised with what comes back.

Find people who can help

As discussed in Chapter 5, you can also find people working in your target companies via Facebook. Searching for "people who work at [Company A]" will bring up a list of profiles belonging to people who have listed their current employer in their "About" section. You can click on their profiles and see if you have any mutual friends whom you could ask to make an introduction. This feature is particularly useful if you are interested in finding out more about a company, to help you to get an insight into its culture or learn about its hiring processes.

Pinterest

Pinterest may not be the first social media channel that springs to mind when thinking of your job search. However, it can enhance your online branding efforts, so it provides a creative way of showing employers who you are. The site is simple to use and growing in popularity, with over 70 million users worldwide.[13]

Set-up

Pinterest is a virtual "bulletin board", allowing you to create a visual repository of images and links that interest you. Creating a profile is as easy as registering with an email address and password – or using another social media account like Facebook or Twitter – and then starting to "pin" images to boards you create. You can include a profile photo and write a brief description of yourself in the "About me" section. As with Twitter, the tone here is friendly and informal. Make sure to integrate a few of your keywords into your profile description so that there is a consistent message across all your social media profiles.

Pinterest boards

You can set up boards, like online cork pinboards, according to different themes that are of interest to you. It's best to create distinct categories instead of generalising. For example, you could create categories named "Great logos", "Website themes" and "Favourite fonts". Your goal is to be professional, but also purposeful and personal. You need to make sure you fill each category with pins that actually align specifically with that category. This will make it easier for you to give specific information about yourself through your choice of pins.

Employer's view: Rachel Kneen, Social Media Manager at O2 (Telefonica UK)

Pinterest has one of the highest click-through rates from pins to websites of any social media platform – but it's about using it for the right reasons. It's huge in the creative industries – the wedding industry, interior design – it's a great way to showcase what you can do. But it's also about balancing your Pinterest profile in and among your other social media efforts.

You can follow other people's accounts or individual boards, and this can be a great source of information. You may find people in the same field as you or people who share the type of content you like. You can choose to follow either the whole account or individual boards as you see fit. Use the search feature to look for keywords that relate to your industry, passion and categories, and you'll almost always find something that pertains to you and is worth pinning. For instance, a very basic search of "mobile apps" brings up dozens of infographics on the subject that will be of interest not only to you but also to your Pinterest followers.

Focus on following

Pinterest is a great site for curating very specifically categorised content, and it allows you to create multiple boards to ensure that you're viewing and sharing a wide variety of content with the least amount of effort. What's great about Pinterest is that lots of other "pinners" are doing your work for you, or at least with you. By following boards run by people who share the same interests and post quality content as well, you cut your work in half when you re-pin their pins. Likewise, when you become an active and expert curator, other pinners will follow you and repin your pins.

Pinning

Keep your pinboard categories in mind, and always be on the lookout for quality content with which to fill them. You can download the Pinterest add-on to your desktop so that whenever you're reading something interesting online, you can choose to pin it to your board. This is an easy way to contribute new material to Pinterest, and it can gain followers for your profile.

Instagram

Instagram is a photo-sharing site. To set up an account, go to https://instagram.com and create an account by inputting your email address and creating a username and password. Instagram will show you people that you know who are already on the platform, and you can start following them to see what your friends and acquaintances are sharing. Click the "Explore" tab to run a keyword search for themes of interest and to find the accounts of people who are sharing images that you find interesting. Instagram shows you photographs on the home page that are based on the accounts you follow and the type of images you have liked on the site. Click on a photo you like and see who posted it, then look at that account, and if it has a number of photographs that appeal to you, consider following the person.

Posting and interacting

Instagram is very simple to use. You can easily upload photographs from your smartphone to the app. You then have a range of filters you can choose from to enhance your photograph, and then you click "Post". Images that show your world and showcase your interests can help to support your online brand. One thing that will do you no favours, unless you are aiming for a career in modelling or on TV, is a barrage of selfies. This could make you come across as being very self-absorbed, which is not high on employers' wish lists.

You can also write descriptive text to go along with your image. Although hashtags are a Twitter-based phenomenon, they have migrated over to Instagram, and users can hashtag their photographs to help them to be discovered. As an example, if you wanted to work in set design, you could post a photograph of a set you helped to create for a university play, and write, "The set I designed with @friendsname is coming together nicely ahead of this weekend's show! #set #stage #theatre #design". A quick browse through other people's images will give you lots of ideas about whats pictures you could post and where to include hashtags.

You can interact with other people's images by clicking the heart icon to indicate that you like them, and you can also comment on them. Again, similarly to Twitter, you can tag people in your images or comments by including their Instagram name in any text that you write.

Video CVs

Video CVs aren't technically social media, but you can share a great video CV via your social profiles. If you make a particularly entertaining and engaging video, it could be noticed online and bring you to the attention of companies who are hiring.

Advantages of making a video CV

The video CV is a really interesting way to show people who you are in a more personalised way than is possible on the written page. Video CVs also provide an opportunity to showcase your creativity and make it work to your advantage. The challenge is to create one that doesn't make employers reach for the "Stop" button after only a few seconds.

Animated video CVs

There are a growing number of very user-friendly, free websites where you can create your own animated video CV. If you're feeling camera-shy or feel that you would like to create something a bit different, these are worth a look. Sites like www.powtoon.com and www.wideo.co have a range of video styles and animations that you can put together to create a great alternative to a written CV. You can personalise your videos further by adding your own images and recording your own script as a voiceover. The platforms provide plenty of tips on how to create your animated video CV. They're a fun way of showcasing your brand, and you can upload your video to YouTube® and share links to that via your social media bios and status updates. You never know – if you make a particularly original video CV, it could get you spotted and lead to some interesting opportunities.

The key elements of a great video CV

The following guidelines will ensure that you plan, record and submit a noteworthy video CV that catches employers' attention in all the right ways.

Prepare before you press record Preparation is the first step to recording a great video CV. Know what you're going to say and the order you're going to say it in, and take the time to say it a few times as you practise in order to get things right.

Set the tone Dress appropriately for the environment in which you want to work. If your desired employers tend to be more on the formal side in tone, dress as if you were attending a face-to-face interview. If you're going for companies with a more relaxed dress code, casual clothes can work well. Consider the lighting as well. Whether you're filming in an office or in a park, a well-lit setting where you can clearly be seen is important. There's no point in making a great video if people can't actually see you. Have the right equipment on hand, set the lighting properly, check the sound and make your video presentations as professional as you would in a face-to-face meeting.

Practice makes perfect Unlike a Skype® chat or video interview, you're making a recording on your own terms, which allows you to practise until you record a video CV that you're happy to share. Keep the video running while you're practising, because you never know which "take" will be your favourite. If you trust someone's professional and personal expertise, have a friend on hand to record you while you're speaking, and this person can offer feedback in between taping sessions.

Keep things brief People's attention spans are short, and recruiters don't have a huge amount of time to make decisions regarding who to call for an interview and who to delete. Keep your video CV under two minutes, ideally. That's plenty of time to communicate your message clearly and concisely.

Be yourself Video CVs are an original way to show people your personality. If you find it hard to show who you are in writing, a good video CV can be a great addition to your online brand. Whatever you do, don't pretend to be something you're not. Faking it will only lead to a mismatch between you and the company, which will quickly become clear at interview, so save everybody time by being genuine. Being yourself also involves not being afraid to show all that you have to offer. This is not the time to be shy.

The best thing to do before you get started is to look at some video CVs, assess what you like and don't like, and then come up with your own unique approach. After all, you are presenting yourself, not a copy of someone else. Watch a few video CVs and do the following exercise to give you some ideas about the elements you would like in your video CV.

Exercise: Video CV review

Log onto a video sharing site like YouTube or Vimeo® and search for "video CV". You could also include a career keyword if you're targeting a particular industry, e.g. "video CV marketing". Watch two video CVs and note down what you like and don't like about each one in the following tables. This should help you to think about what you do – and don't – want to include in your video CV.

	What I liked	What I didn't like
Video CV 1		
Video CV 2		

Once you've planned out your content and locations and had a go at making a video CV, show it to a few friends to get their feedback before putting it online. You want people to notice and share it for the right reasons, so getting other people to have a look and give their impressions is an important quality control step to take before you upload your video CV online.

What to do next

If you feel confident about the ways that you can use social media to help you in your job search, get online and start managing your profiles. If you're feeling unsure about what you would like to highlight, revisit Chapter 2 to remind yourself what you have to say.

Chapter 9

Useful websites

http://blogs.techsmith.com/category/tips-how-tos/
This site's "Tips and How Tos" section is full of helpful ideas and advice that you can use to create a great video CV.
https://vimeo.com and **www.youtube.com** These two video sharing sites have a large number of video CVs on their pages; you can search for "video CV" and be inspired.
www.about.com This is where you can find numerous articles on using social media, including Facebook, in your job search.

References

Introduction

1. "How Recruiters Use Social Networks to Make Hiring Decisions Now"' at http://business.time.com/2012/07/09/how-recruiters-use-social-networks-to-make-hiring-decisions-now/
2. "Getting hired in a digital world" at http://careerenlightenment .com/infographic-getting-hired-digital-world

Chapter 4

3. "How EY use Facebook to recruit professionals: Case study" at http://linkhumans.com/blog/twitter/how-ernst-young-use-facebook-to-recruit-professionals-case-study
4. "Mars unleashes Twitter Graduate Recruitment Drive" at http://www.themanufacturer.com/articles/mars-unleashes-twitter-graduate-recruitment-drive/
5. "'My Marriot Hotel' opens its doors on Facebook" at http://news.marriott.com/2011/06/my-marriott-hotel-opens-its-doors-on-facebook.html
6. "Navy attempting to recruit cryptologists through Facebook game" at http://www.telegraph.co.uk/news/worldnews/northamerica/usa/10799470/US-Navy-attempting-to-recruit-cryptologists-through-Facebook-game.html
7. "Announcing Starfighter" at http://www.kalzumeus.com/2015/03/09/announcing-starfighter/

Chapter 6

8. "The social recruiting pocket guide" at http://socialmeep.com/infographic-the-social-recruiting-pocket-guide/

9. "The Effect of LinkedIn on Deception in Resumes" at https://blogs. cornell.edu/socialmedialab/files/2014/01/2012-Guillory-Hancock-Effect-of-LinkedIn-on-deception-in-resumes.pdf
10. http://www.slideshare.net/afvh/the-linkedin-guide-to-the-perfect-work-self

Chapter 9

11. "The Top 20 Valuable Facebook Statistics – Updated May 2015" at https://zephoria.com/top-15-valuable-facebook-statistics/
12. Expanded ramblings at www.expandedramblings.com

Index